Songs of Hope

JERRY GOEBEL

For information contact:
Brother Blue Publishing
POBox 50395
Washington, DC 20091
BrotherBluePublishing.com

Cover Photography: Christine Henry
Cover Design: Pete Morelewicz
Interior Design: Gene Monterastelli

Manufactured in the United States of America

TABLE OF CONTENTS

Forward

     I never intended to publish the book you are holding in your hands. You need to understand I am a dreamer and a planner. There never seems to be enough hours in the day or days in the week to do all the things I want to do. I carry around in my pocket a list of dreams I would like to chase, if I only had the time. I am not complaining. I know I am blessed not only to have dreams, but the opportunities to chase them. I am sharing this only to illustrate how odd it would be that I would find myself investing so much time and energy in to something I had no plans for.

     I found myself in the Fall of 2003 sitting in a coffee shop south of Baltimore sitting across the table from Jerry. Jerry was in town to do some work at two parishes and to work with a prison in the area. At this point I don't if I would be lucky enough to describe Jerry as a friend. (I definitely do now.) I knew Jerry professionally and it would be a great honor to be considered a professional peer of his. Over twenty years ago, Jerry was doing the type of work I do now, traveling from place to place sharing the Gospel message with young people through entertainment and stories (the only difference Jerry is a musician and I am a juggler). When Jerry started, there was no infrastructure for our type of work. Not only did Jerry have to convince others that he was effective at his craft, but that his craft was important. Because of the hard work of Jerry and many like him (such as Tom Franzak), twenty years later when the ministry I am blessed to be a part of started, we were only have to convince people that we were proficient at our craft, for they understood the impact of entertainment ministries. For this reason, even before I met him, I understood I owed a great debt to Jerry.

     My admiration for Jerry stems from more than the fact I understand I owe him a professional debt. You see, when ever I am describing Jerry Goebel to someone who doesn't know him, I generally go on and on about all the wonderful work he had done with the homeless and youth and gangs and prisoners and the dieing. Then I pause, as who ever I am talking to starts to glaze over. I take deep breath and say, "He is who I want to be when I grow up." Jerry is a model of what it means to live the Gospel message a radical way.

     Unfortunately, I think "living the Gospel in a radical way" has become the victim of punch-less rhetoric. It is a rallying call we hear from the pulpit. It is something we pay lip service to. But, in the end, so often, it ends up being nothing more than a slogan on the back of a t-shirt. We are suppose say we are "living radical Christian lives", but what does that have to do with me when I am plopped in front of the TV watching an episode of The Simpson's? It is as if "radical Christian living" is an activity we do at certain time and certain places opposed to a lifestyle. The reason I want to be like Jerry when I grow up is because Jerry is living a radical Christian life.

     At this point in his life Jerry's three primary ministries are working with the homeless, working in the prisons, and providing spiritual direction for the sick, the dieing, and their families. As you can image these are not paying jobs. So, on the side he continues to travel, preaching and singing. Between these gigs, the jewelry his wife makes, and donation the family some how manages to make ends meet. I don't know if Jerry would ever admit it, but I have a feeling that they truly live month to month. Jerry (and his family) is living on the edge because he is so convicted by the Gospel message. I love getting e-mail from Jerry, because with out trying, they preach the Gospel message. A message will matter-of-factly say: "Gene, Hope you are well. It was a great day. Three of the guys from the homeless shelter came with me to the prison to do ministry." Or an apology which read: "Gene, Sorry to not have the edit to you when I promised. A woman I have been working with, who had cancer, died last night. I have spent most of the day praying with the family and helping them to plan the funeral." That is Jerry's daily life. That is living a radical Christian life.

     As I was saying, I was sitting in this coffee shop with Jerry. He is sharing with me the story of a 20 year old that is on death row. How Jerry tells the story, the kid (sure he is an adult, but really he is a kid) should have been off death row a long time ago, but because of some legal issues, it wasn't happening. Jerry shared how the young man is actually happy that he is still on death row. Not because is looking to die, but in his time on death row he has started a bible study for the other prisoners. (His own conversion came in prison.) The way he sees it, if he wasn't still on death row, he wouldn't have this chance to share the Gospel message. I was blown away and speechless. I have heard the "preach to the prisoners" my whole life, but not from someone who was doing it.

I then asked Jerry a simple question, "How can I support you?" At this point in my life I was kicking around the idea of publish a book or two. I had done some limited research in to how a book gets made (right down to the Cub Scout style tour of a printing plant near my house). In my mind, I thought I basically could pull off the printing of a book. Jerry for many years had been writing bible studies for his digital news letter and web site, so we thought an easy project would be to take some of his writings and publish them in hopes of raising a little money to support his family. If he provided the writing, I would provide the time and energy to put the book together and the credit card to pay for it (because I didn't have four thousand dollars on hand). Our time together ended. As I was driving away, it dawned on my, I had just committed to publish a book. Something I had never done before and something I had no idea how much time and effort it would take to do. (In retrospect, my best guess was a wild under estimation.)

In the months that followed, I have tried to understand what compelled me to help with this project (and what has given me the strength to persevere). After a lot of thought it came to me. The reason that I wanted so desperately to help Jerry is because I understand that I am not brave enough (at least not yet) the live the Gospel message in the radical way Jerry does. I think by saying, "Jerry is who I want to be when I grow up," it is my way of justify the fact that I am not living that way right now. It helps me to rationalize my life, by making it something I am going to grow in to at a later date.

If you have never been blessed to meet Jerry, you are about to meet him in a very personal way. In the pages that follow are his reflections on Psalms. (He actually wrote on 150 of them, and hopefully we have selected some of the best reflections.) These reflections were written as he worked with the youth of the Yakama Valley. Many of them in gangs, on the verge of joining gangs, and (because of Jerry and others work and perseverance) on their way out of gangs. These writings share his experience with these youth, his family, his own struggle as pilgrim, and the challenges of daily life.

I think it is very important that I warn you. These writing are going to make you very uncomfortable. These writings are going to make you stretch. These writings are going to challenge the way you live your life. But, all of this is going to happen in a good way. In these pages you will find a testament to the Living God who is ever present in our lives that we so often miss.

It has been a true blessing to be a part of this project, for it has forced me to shine light in to my own life and on to my own actions. I do full time ministry, so it is easy to get wrapped up in the idea that I am living a radical Christian life. In reality, I am simply a pilgrim like everyone else. Doing the best I can. Trying to grow closer to my God and the Body of Christ, which is His people on this earth. These writing continue to help me to do just that. They have helped given me find hope in the faithfulness of Our Lord, as well as challenged me to continue to meet that Lord in all those around me, especially the poorest of the poor. My prayer for you is that in these words, in some small, Our Lord will speak to you in the way that He has spoken to me.

Finally, I have one request of you. Please keep Jerry, his family, and those he ministers to in your prayers.

¡Que Dios te bendiga!

Gene Monterastelli
Publisher
April 2004

Songs of Hope

A Tree Firmly Planted
Psalm 1

They are like a tree
planted near streams of water,
that yields its fruit in season;
Its leaves never wither;
whatever they do prospers
Psalm 1:3

I love the sound of flowing water. From the crashing thunder of waves to the silent trickle of a stream. Water quiets the restless soul and stills the frantic mind. It leads to a respectful silence that is often primed for prayer.

Normally, I am not the quiet sort. I was born busy. My energy turned on and off in increments of one hundred percent. Like a toggle switch instead of a dimmer switch - I was either running flat out or lying flat out. The ultimate curse my mother could import upon me was, "I hope you have children who are just like you."

I am certainly not alone in the curse of "busy-ness." We live in a frenetic culture that equates the thickness of our calendar books with our personal value. If we aren't on call or online, then we must be out of touch and off the scene. Beepers are a highly-prized Christmas present for many of our nation's teens, as are mobile phones - while many schools have now created policies to prevent their use in the classroom. In the check-out lines at stores, one can't help but notice the plethora of twenty, five and even two-minute cookbooks. On the back of our racing mini-vans and suburban assault vehicles is the popular bumper sticker, "Mom's Taxi" (signifying the race from one school event to another). At home, we gather around the microwave to eat in tides so as to accommodate our frenetic pace; one family member washes in as another family member is pulled out into a never-ending sea of frenzy.

Still, all our rush has done little to bring us meaning, purpose or a sense of reason. Instead, it leaves us feeling grouchy, tired and empty.
It's difficult to balance this busy-ness I see around me with my call as a missionary. All too often, I sit by a person in a hospital or nursing home who laments the time they have wasted on things of little importance - when those things are viewed through the hues of imminent death. All too often, that wasted time was at work; striving for money, titles or possessions. All too often, their singular wish would be to recapture some of those spent moments and invest them instead with children or other loved ones.

Perhaps it is just the land-locked people I know in the middle of this desert country, but I've been interested to hear how many people - when they talk about happier memories - often refer to family times that revolve around water. They discuss escapes to the beach, a lake or camp-outs by a stream.

"Like a tree planted by streams," states the Psalmist. Perhaps we should think about capturing some 'Water-Time' soon. It's not just "the water" that counts - it is the intentional time out of busy-ness; the intentional commitment of taking time to slow down and listen to God.

The Psalms were written about just such 'Water-Times'. Throughout this book you will find stories of men blessed and cursed. Those cursed are like 'bones in the wasteland,' those blessed are like 'streams in desert.' Throughout this book, we find that blessing in direct correlation to closeness to God; "Water-Time."
The New Testament uses two words for blessing. One means you are blessed by your circumstances (Blessed are the meek). The other term means you are blessed for what you did with your circumstances. This word is eulogeo, from which we get the word eulogy. It means the summary of your life.
The clear question throughout the Psalms is this: Have I taken my circumstances (my desert or wasteland) and made a blessing out of it (a living steam)? On this day, at this moment; am I closer to a dry bone lifeless in the desolation or a stream giving life in desert?

God is offering that blessing; to be our source of water in all seasons. A theme continued by Jesus who proclaims to be living water. My ability to be blessed and to be a blessing is in direct correlation to my closeness to the Living Water.
Where am I planted today?

It is the joy of the Master Gardener to - at any time - plant us closely and firmly by his living waters. Let's seize our 'Water-Time' now. Let us seek this source of life even before we close this reading.

Lord, plant me firmly in your living waters. Quench my thirst, restore my dry bones, make me a source of living hope to all who find me in their desert. Let me know that I am called to be blessed (circumstance) and to be a blessing to others (eulogy) throughout my life.

God is in my interruptions
Psalm 80

LORD of hosts, restore us;
let your face shine upon us,
that we may be saved.
                    Psalm 80:20

I saw God's face yesterday. Three times he appeared to me and I nearly missed him. It wasn't until I finally collected my thoughts this morning that I recognized his features.

As I write this, I am on an airplane. I am taking a group of fourteen people to an orphanage in Mexico. Needless to say, yesterday (my last day of preparation for the trip) was a busy day. It was not just the final packing and flurry of phone calls from nervous participants and parents. There were also a number of emergency events that needed immediate attention.

A woman I'd been visiting at the rest home passed away and her sister asked if I would do the funeral. The poor lady had lived a hard life and died a painful and drawn-out death. I had been visiting her since my arrival and was honored to have helped her through those passing moments.

Before leaving for the funeral (it was in the next town over), I received a phone call from a young man who was recently out of prison and had been referred to me. He was 19 and had been in the adult penal system since he was fifteen. Recently paroled, he had fallen back into the same patterns with the same gang that he had promised to avoid. He had disappeared from my radar screen for several days and when he finally resurfaced he was in trouble again. I went straight from the funeral to the courtroom and sat through the fears, the concerns and pain of his morning.

By the time I made it back to church, my task list was growing into an ugly, overwhelming beast. No whip or bull prod was going to tame this monster. I considered setting fire to my desk, but I'd just changed the furniture around in my office and didn't want to char my printer. I thought, "maybe a few strategically placed Claymores would get rid of the paper behemoth. Instead my friend, Deanne, decided to drop by at that precise moment.

Deanne comes in like clockwork. Whether or not I am with someone, she comes into my office and closes the door (which has really exacerbated some other people who've come to visit me when Deanne dropped by).

Deanne deals with horrific demons. Depression and paranoia overwhelm her. For the last few weeks she has been afraid to walk across her doorstep because she believes that the neighbors buried someone under it. She wants me to dig it up and look for the body. I'd do it, but last month she was convinced there was a body in the Mayor's car and wanted me to break into it as well.

She comes in weekly for prayer and I love her dearly. Despite her absolute poverty, she has never asked for a dime. We pray, she drinks a glass of water and then asks to lay down in a corner of my office and rest for awhile.

On this day, Deanne was making herself physically ill over my Mexico trip. She was sure that the plane would not make it and that - even if it did - I would be abducted by street gangs upon stepping out onto the streets of Mexico City. (At this present moment, 32,000 feet in the air, I am choosing to not focus on Deanne's fears).

After Deanne left, I reluctantly turned back to the task list and realized we were no longer even in the same weight class. I did the only respectable thing - I decided to sneak out of the ring. I left my windows open so that, prayerfully, a tornado would come by and suck all those evil papers over the rainbow. The weight of that pile would easily smash a wicked witch or two.

Sitting next to my wife on the flight this morning, I began to share some of the highlights of my previous day. I wasn't complaining about it, in fact, I was honored by the people who put their confidence in me. That's when the face of God started to become clearer to me: In the face of a grieving woman who lost her sister; in the eyes of a scared, young man fearing internment; in the pleas of a woman challenged by exceptional fear. All day long, I'd been praying to a distant God, missing his eyes as they stared right into mine. It was as though I'd been using the phone to speak to a loved one in the same room.

God's face is near. I need to work at recognizing that God is in my interruptions. I need to become more adept at seeing his features in the intense eyes of sorrow, fear and loneliness that stare at me everyday.

Give me practiced eyes that will attune to your features, Lord. Give me awareness of your presence, the desire to seek your face and the faith to believe you will present yourself - Amen.

Consistent in Death

Psalm 22

My God, my God, why have you abandoned me?
Psalm 22:2a

There have been many times that I have sat by the deathbed of a Believer awaiting with them the passage into their new life. Frequently, I have read the Psalms watching my weakened friend mouth a word or a verse with me. Not having strength to recite the entire Psalm, a word or two is enough to carry and comfort their heart.

Most of us recognize the words of this Psalm as some of the last utterances of Jesus Christ (Mark 15:34 and Matthew 27:46). Some believe that these words indicate Christ's feelings of abandonment and complete isolation as he died a tortuous death on the cross.

However, these words are also the first words of the 22nd Psalm. It is highly plausible that Jesus was praying the Psalms as he sought relief from his physical agony. He had learned these words as early as five and was most likely able to repeat them by heart. When we read this Psalm it provides us a deep insight into the depth of Jesus' faith and his absolute trust in the Father's power during his last few moments in his temporal body. Far from a gasp of utter abandonment, this was the beginning of a prayer for comfort and deliverance.

Two other important lines in the Psalm read: "But you, O Lord, be not far off; O my strength come quickly to help me" (v. 19), and; "For He has not despisedm or disdained the suffering of the afflicted one; He has not hidden His face from Him but has listened to his cry for help." (v. 24)

Facing the cruelty of man and the gates of hell; Christ did not end His earthly life any different than He lived it. He did not draw a final breath of despondency, wondering if the Father had abandoned or forgotten Him. Dying as He lived, Christ's final breath was a prayer - the prayer of the suffering servant. Turning to God (by reciting a poem He would have learned in His childhood) Jesus shows us the way to cross the bridge into suffering and death as surely as He showed us how to live.

"Come and see," you told your Disciples. Every instance of your life was an invitation to know God by knowing you. You lived the example of loving faith - and you modeled it in your dying. Lord, help us turn to you in every situation. Help us long for an understanding of your Word that we might know your example and your comfort clearly - Amen.

The foggy path
Psalm 97

Cloud and darkness surround the Lord;
justice and right are the foundation of his throne.
Psalm 97:2

There's a line in the first Indiana Jones movie that always makes me chuckle. Indy is attempting to catch the Ark of the Covenant as it races off in the back of a Nazi truck. He sends his compadres off in multiple directions to prepare to re-capture the treasure. However, one assistant asks; "What are you going to do now?"

Without hesitation, Indy responds with; "Don't ask me, I'm making this up as I go along."

This quip touches my funny bone because it sums up so much of my life - especially since I entered mission-work full-time. There are so many circumstances in which I find myself for which I could never have been prepared. Holding an abused child, standing by a young teenage girl seeking a way out of a gang, praying with a young man whose family is torn apart by chemical and physical abuse. Three-fourths of the time I feel like Indy; that I am also making it up as I go along.

In Exodus 19:9 there is a short piece of scripture which I cherish: The Lord said to Moses, "I am going to come to you in a cloud..."

It makes me wonder if perhaps this is always going to be the state of a Christian leader. Perhaps Christ-centered leaders need to be so far out on the edge of life that they are consistently wondering what to say or do next. Together, we may be little more than a people constantly looking for ways to bring Christ's healing touch to a terribly confused and foggy world.

My experience teaches me that there are no road maps where we are called to serve - only compass points. Like constellations of stars, we are led by points of light that indicate where the Spirit leads - if we are attuned to her. However, one thing does become exceedingly clear in the fog - we cannot rely on ourselves and must turn to God for direction. In fact, our greatest power can flow from the dependency that is created when we operate in the confusion of the fog. We are at our weakest - but God is at His greatest.

Perhaps, active believers should accept that we must always be one step beyond our ability to take control. It would force us to rely on his call instead of our comfort. Is it possible that our most appropriate motto may be; "I don't know, I'm making it up as I go along."

"...and the Lord came to him in a thick cloud."

Give us the courage, Lord, to live beyond our comfort zone. Seeking to apply your Gospel to the injustice of this world is confusing, difficult and often overwhelming. Help us recognize that even though we might be lost in the fog - you are not. That is when we need to listen most for your call.

My shield and glory
Psalm 3

But you, LORD, are a shield around me;
my glory, you keep my head high.
Psalm 3:4

When I was a little boy I had a small brown border collie named Fawn. We gave her this name because her beautiful colors looked like those of a baby deer. I loved Fawn and we were inseparable, pursuing all of our adventures together, whether it be battling pirates or dodging arrows. Wherever I was, Fawn was there as well.

Growing up the son of a forester meant that I spent a great deal of time outdoors. Daily I would explore a part of the thousands of acres of National Forest that we were privileged to call our backyard. On one of these childhood explorations, I remember being quite distant from my house when I heard a rustling in the bushes beside me. There have been times when fear has challenged me throughout my life, but (to a fault) my desire to 'know' always exceeded my ability to reason. If I had been born a cat, I would have been the one that curiosity killed and killed and killed and (repeat up to nine lives).

Dropping to my hands and knees I began to scout around for what was making the shuffling sound. Much to my surprise - and terror - I came nose to nose with a huge, cranky porcupine. I had not even begun to grind my body into hyper-reverse when a brown shot came flying from my right directly into the mass of quills. It was Fawn. Head first, she took the barbs right in her face while I backed first into a tree, then turn and ran headlong through the brambles.

When I was able to pick up Fawn, her poor muzzle was a mass of quills. I remember crying while my father painstakingly pulled out each one, one at a time. With barely a whimper the poor animal lay trembling in fear and pain across a picnic table.

God said He would be our shield. He did not say that he would send a shield so that we might defend ourselves: He would be our shield! He would personally defend us. God is not an adoring fan. He does not watch from the boxed owner's bleacher in the height of Heaven's stadium. When we turn to him, he takes our side and goes straight into the battle.

Just as Fawn took on the porcupine and absorbed its sharp quills so that I could escape; our God - through his only begotten son - took a crown of pointed thorns and bore our pain.

He did not send a shield - He became a shield.

Lord, I am mindful of my sin, please keep me mindful of your mercy. You did not *send* a shield to protect me; rather, you became a living shield through the loving sacrifice of your son, Jesus Christ. Thank you. - Amen

"I am clothed in my own majesty."
Psalm 93

The LORD is king, robed with majesty;
the LORD is robed, girded with might.
The world will surely stand in place,
never to be moved.

Psalm 93:1

I was once in a church where the Pastor seemed to believe that he was the 'Lord' who is referred to in this verse. A slight change in the words would have fit this man perfectly: "In his mind he reigns. He is wrapped in his own sense of majesty and armed with belligerence. His mind is firmly established and cannot be moved."

If the pastor didn't come up with an idea, you had better allow him to think he did - or it would not be worthy of his consideration. As for his actions, he was far above explaining his decisions to others. Conflict resolution meant he was right and you were too tired to argue about it anymore.

When people who behave in this manner have a little power behind their positions - they can become quite tyrannical. They turn into unbearable bosses, parents, board members or dictators. In my situation, things became so bad that I was ready to quit my job. However, I realized how much I would miss the ministry in which I was involved and that the one's I would hurt would only be those with whom I had been able to develop a bond of trust.

I began to sense God working on my perspective, even on the subject of my prayer. I had been praying that God would change 'him' - the person that I thought was the cause of my problems. I had been asking God to alter the 'circumstances' in which I found myself, my 'situation'. Slowly - with God's love - instead of praying for the perfect boss, the perfect situation, or the perfect circumstance, I began to see Jesus on the cross. In his sacrifice, I could learn how holiness is responding 'perfectly' to imperfect people, situations and circumstances.

My prayer became, "Change me, O Lord." "Change my heart, my attitude and my responses."

Faith grows as it overcomes obstacles and daily struggles - not when it avoids them. Faith leads us to realize that there is only One who truly reigns. There is only One who is "robed in majesty, armed with strength, firmly established and who cannot be moved." If I truly believe this, then, I must also believe that he has placed me here - in these circumstances - for his purposes and to a greater glory.

Jesus, please don't make our circumstances easier, make our character stronger.

Childlike Distance

Psalm 53

They have good reason to fear,
though now they do not fear.
For God will certainly scatter
the bones of the godless.
They will surely be put to shame,
for God has rejected them.

Psalm 53:6

When I was a child, the further I went from my parents the more shadows looked like monsters, sounds made noise like wild animals and unfamiliar objects became vicious strangers.

As an adult, I have failed to leave this infantile interpretation of the world. However, it's not my earthly father's distance that causes me to fret. It is the distance I am from my heavenly Father.

When I am distant from Him, my anxiety knows no bounds. I worry about what other people might say about me. I become over-concerned about my job. As I become more wary I become wearier as fear drains away my joy. When I am distant from my heavenly Father, the things that I face are overwhelming problems instead of challenges - opportunities for spiritual growth.

It seems as though I have not changed much since childhood. The things that I fear have changed but not the basic fear itself. I moved from fearing monsters to fearing overwhelming tasks or overbearing people. And, the proportion of those fears grows in perfect step with my distance from the Father. I become like the object of the Psalmist's lesson: "Here they were overwhelmed with dread when there was nothing to dread."

My single solution, as an adult, is also no different than my solution as a child. I need to run back to my Father, into the folds of His embrace. That is the only place where we - God's creation - were destined to find peace.

Lord, recover me from my distance from your love - your path. In that distance I become so lost, so unhealthy, so fearful. My hope lies only in you, my Creator and my Father. Bring me back, Lord. Show me a light, keep me on a steady course towards your embrace - Amen.

Shepherd King
Psalm 23

The LORD is my shepherd;
there is nothing I lack.
Psalm 23:1

From the days of David to the days of Christ, the shepherd's crook was never seen as a cute toy or bejeweled ornament - especially by wayward sheep or unwelcome visitors. It was certainly not decorative or symbolic as it has become today through the gold-enhanced staffs carried by Bishops of many denominations. The long, straight end was most often used to "whack" sheep into order. It was also used as a weapon against multiple predators attracted to sheep. The "hook" was a handy tool utilized for "yanking" wayward sheep out of the brambles.

It is somewhat embarrassing for us to realize that if God is the protective shepherd that makes us the dim-witted sheep. This is not exactly an overwhelming compliment. Sheep are not judged by their intelligence, they were easily distracted followers. Unruly and readily overwhelmed by terror - an isolated sheep will often fall over and die rather than run from significant danger.

At the same time, shepherds were not high on the Jewish social list. They spent months, with their animals, living in the rugged wilderness. They slept on the ground, right in the entryways of their hand-built, bramble-bush sheep pens. They fought deftly - and often - for the grazing and watering rights of their furry charges. Worst of all - in the Jewish mind - they worked on the Sabbath. Their flock and their responsibilities simply would not allow them to do otherwise.

Yet, the shepherd knew his own. They were regarded as the epitome of compassion. Their faithfulness and commitment to their charges was recognized as being without comparison. Most important, David, who had written and compiled many of these Psalms, was himself a shepherd. That was long before he became the greatest earthly king Israel was to ever know.

We are the sheep; sometimes stupid, often wandering. Jesus is the Shepherd; doing whatever it takes to bring us safely back to green pastures. He cares for us with diligence, wanting no sheep to remain lost; searching every thicket, crevasse or mountain until we are brought safely home. When we are well, He leads us to safe pastures and restful waters - when we are weary, crippled or ill, He carries us on His shoulders.

It was those same shoulders that were stretched to breaking by a cross. They are also the shoulders where our burdens will - once and for all time - find eternal comfort and rest.

Dear Shepherd King, thank you for your commitment to this wandering flock. When I am too weary to walk, let me trust in your strength, when I am too confused to find the way, let me listen for your call, when I am too crippled to continue, let me sleep on your shoulders. Thank you, my Shepherd King - Amen.

A mouse for my wife

Psalm 21

LORD, the king finds joy in your power;
in your victory how greatly he rejoices!
Psalm 21:2

My wife stepped out on the front porch to pick up the morning paper. No sooner had she opened the door than I heard a shriek. The cat did it again... She was a true "mouser" (the cat that is - not my wife) and she seemed to believe that we had to approve of her catches. Her feline cognition operated under the misconception that my wife's screams were indications of parental approval. Never, would the ferocious feline register that there might be a reason why a rousing chorus of "Hail the Conquering Hero" would never accompany her victories over the tyranny of Mousedom. The cat had a 'genetically ordained' concept of victory to which my wife was 'genetically averse'.

Often, I totally miss the victories that God longs to share in my life. My concept of victory and God's concept of victory seem comparable to that of my cat and my wife. Like my cat laying a mouse on the doorstep, I naively think that God will be unimaginably proud of me when I lay my achievements before Him.

But God doesn't seem to want my accomplishments. Nor, does He want my things, my earnings, my incredibly witty thoughts or rousing speeches.
He wants my heart.

The God who favored the widow's mite cares not for the amount that is offered, but only for the heart that is offering. He wants my heart, not my toys. He wants my belief, my desires, my hopes, and my wonder. It is not what I do that pleases Him, it is who I am that brings Him joy. It is not the 'victories' that I lay on his doorstep which he relishes. Instead, it is the sins that I bring before Him in the simple hope of salvation.

Lord, make me victorious in your eyes. Bring me back to Human 'Beingness' as I strive towards Human Havingness or Human Doingness. Let me worth be found in my consistent and transparent availability to you.

"I told you so!"

Psalm 7

They open a hole and dig it deep,
but fall into the pit they have dug.
Psalm 7:16

The worst four words in the English language may well be, "I told you so." How does one respond to a statement like that? Should you say: "Gee, I'm so glad you are so smart;" "Thank you for your gracious and moving support;" or, "May God continue to bless you with such incredibly accurate hindsight."

My father was a forester and thus, I spent a great deal of my youth living in forests. When I was about seven, I read a book about a boy who made friends with a huge bear. As a result of that book, I became determined to catch a bear and make him my life-long companion. I ran to my dad and told him that I must have a shovel right away, sharing with him the grand purpose behind my zeal. He smiled and without commenting handed me a spade.

I spent the better part of that day digging a hole very wide and very deep. Eventually, I was throwing dirt as high as I could in order to get it out of the top of the hole. Eventually, the hole was so deep that I wound up catching something very unexpected…

Myself…

I was cold, hungry, tired and very afraid. Believing that - at any moment - some bear was going to fall into the pit with me. In my fear, I remember trying everything to get out. Additional digging only complicated my situation. Attempting to stand on my shovel gave me little advantage but not enough to extricate me from my self-made predicament. I dreaded the inevitable approach of a bear's colossal shadow; darkening the sun, blotting out the sky. I waited, terrified that the bear - spying a little a tasty little tot - would gobble me down like a midday morsel with blond frosting.

Eventually, a shadow did come. I could not see clearly the form behind the huge frame that seemed to blot out all celestial objects. But, finally, gratefully, a familiar voiced boomed forth from the dark mass.

He could have laughed, walked away or said a million snide comments. Instead, he jumped down (actually, more like, stepped down) into the hole and handed me a sandwich. "Thought you might be hungry," was all he said.

He sat with me for awhile. His mouth over-occupied with crunchy peanut butter. Slowly using his tongue to get all the sticky remains from between each tooth. All the while he sized up my hole. He looked carefully at the floor, the walls and the construction in general. Finally, between melodramatic chews, licks and smacks, he drawled, "its a nice hole, do you need some help out?"

What I expected to hear was, "I told you so." It was, in fact, what I deserved. But, grace is what I received. "Do you need some help out?" That was all.

"He who digs a hole and scoops it out falls into the pit he has made," that's what the Psalmist said. But, fortunately, he was writing from an Old Testament Perspective. With the gift of Jesus a new covenant was made. The "I told you so," of legalism instead becomes the, "do you need some help out?" of a compassionate Father.

Thanks, dad; thanks, God.

Lord, if I got what I deserved I would be overwhelmed with hopelessness. But you took my sin and bound it to your Son. He took my sin and unbound me from its curse. On bended knee, with overwhelming gratitude, I give my humble thanks - Amen

Hypothesis or Declaration

Psalm 79

*Lord, inflict on our neighbors sevenfold
the disgrace they inflicted on you.*
Psalm 79:12-13

Then we, your people, the sheep of your pasture, will give thanks to you forever; through all ages we will declare your praise.

There are times when my children will try to barter with me. "Dad, if you take me out for a happy meal, then I'll clean my room." "If you let me watch cartoons, then I'll pick up my dishes."

You would think that my children would learn, after all these years, that this Daddy is not conducive to bartering. In fact, the opposite is really true - it bugs the whiskers off me.

However, I must in humility admit that the apple probably is not falling far from the tree in this trait. More than once I have caught myself playing the same childish game with God. "Lord, if you help me get out of the consequences of my actions, then I'll witness to your power." "If you get me more money, I'll tithe." "Lord, help me get a new car and I'll drive the kids to youth events everywhere."

The Israelites, my children and I, all seem to have fallen into the same mistaken concept. The Israelites statement was: "If you crush my enemies, then I will praise you forever…"

I wonder if God feels somewhat contentious about these statements. I wonder if 'hypothetical' statements of "if, then" bother Him as much as they bother me.

I know, as a parent, that giving into this verbal blackmail might silence a current problem, but it only exacerbates future ones. Leading always to even greater 'if, then' statements. A misguided concept that, "it worked last time, let's up the ante" mindset.

However, faith in God doesn't work like that. It is not emotional or verbal blackmail, it is not a hypothesis. Faith is not a 'if, then' hypothesis, it is a 'because' declaration.

We believe 'because' God loves us. We choose joy 'because' God desires it of us. We are confident 'because' His is the kingdom, the power and the glory.

Faith is not an action /consequence equation or an 'if/then' hypothesis. It is placing ourselves before God, wondering at His awesome power and praising His mighty presence in our lives.

Lord, fill me with expectation. Fill me so high that it washes away my hypothesis-style beliefs. Free me from 'if, then' thinking. Fill me with the daily wonder of 'because'. 'Because' you sent your son to die for me. 'Because' you desire my joy. 'Because' you are our loving Father - Amen

The Sensibly Impaired
Psalm 75

"The earth and all its inhabitants will quake,
but I have firmly set its pillars." Selah
Psalm 75:4

Flying in and out of most southern airports during the summer means you are going to encounter some amount of turbulence. In the late afternoon, the hot air pushes high into the summer sky. It billows into ominous clouds that bulge up against the edge of the atmosphere.

Inside these watery behemoths, the exchange between cold and hot air is as violent as the pounding of heavy artillery.

Even a jumbo jet feels dwarfed and insignificant as it tries to find a safe approach to solid ground through a maze of blackened thunderclouds. As the plane bounces down its glide path, it is always interesting to see the varying responses of the jostled occupants.

Some are in terror, holding on to their armrests as if pulling them up will keep the plane from falling. Some are disgruntled and angry because they cannot read their paper or type on the laptop computers. There are a few who are completely wiped out because they took a couple extra motion sickness pills; when the going got rough - they got sedated. Their eyes can't even open large enough to see if there is any danger around them.

Finally, there are always a small group of strange people who enjoy the ride like it was one giant and massively expensive roller coaster.

Perhaps these people are mentally challenged. They don't seem to understand that there are no strings holding up their streamlined sardine can. Do their brains release too much dopamine? Do they operate under some mistaken belief that life is no more than their own personal amusement park?

Some people view life with fear. Every challenge and obstacle is to be avoided or denied. Some view obstacles as interruptions, diverting them from their agendas, their pre-charted course. Some use alcohol or drugs to deaden the impact of the challenges and interruptions of their life.

Finally, there are these sensibility-impaired individuals who want to make life into a party zone. Each of these types is riding on the same airplane. Each of them is bouncing through the same clouds, facing all the same problems. It just seems that some of them rest in the words of the Psalmist, "when the earth and all its pillars shake, it is you who holds it firm."

Comforted by greater hands, worry simply seems unnatural to them.

Those who greet the flight will experience a variety of passengers. Many will be ashen-faced zombies who wobble free of the ramp with airsickness bags clutched close in hand. Then, there will also be one or two individuals slipping off the plane with silly ear-to-ear grins across their faces, ready to ride the next bronco into the fading sun.

How awesome is your creation, Lord. How wonderful the rules that apply to your universe - both physically and spiritually. We tamper with those rules at our peril. Gravity pulls the smaller bodies towards denser masses as certainly as our souls are pulled towards you. At the center of all this is You, our most holy Creator. Praise your awesome creation, your awesome works - Amen.

Is the super-bowl really super?

Psalm 18

He parted the heavens and came down,
a dark cloud under his feet.
Mounted on a cherub he flew,
borne along on the wings of the wind.
Psalm 18:10-11

My father's vocation and avocation has been caring for the earth, nature has been his canvas and the ways of the forest were his passion. I did not grow up in a house of refined art and music. Our walls were adorned with Sear's finest prints and our halls were filled with both kinds of acceptable music: Country and Western.

Raphael, Matisse, Van Gogh, Picasso, all of these were unfamiliar names to me. I never floated on the strains of Mozart, Beethoven, Gershwin, or Tchaikovsky (except when Walt Disney did an animated version of Peter and the Wolf). Conversely, I could name for you the differences between the pines and the firs, I know which roots are edible and which could kill you. I could read the weather and the footprints of animals in the wet earth. I wondered at the breadth of the stars and was amazed at the fury of a summer thunderstorm and winter blizzard.

The overwhelming beauty of art and the awesome power of nature have become distant to many people. We do not live in a culture of wonder; instead, we choose a culture of immediate and momentary pleasure. In a crazed rush, we ignore the starry sky and neglect the finer subtleties of the Artist's brush. We've traded classic art for cereal box tops and natural wonder for flashy screen savers. We call a repeat performance at the Super Bowl "historic" and mistake pro sports standouts for legends.

In a world where the phrase "miraculous" is used by sportscasters for each slam dunk, home run or long bomb; it is not hard to realize why we have lost a sense of eternal awe. But His glory will only wait so long. Someday, perhaps soon, he will again "part the heavens and come down." Once again he will have "dark clouds under his feet." He will be "mounted on the cherubim flying; soaring on the wings of the wind." At that time, we will stand in awe, glorifying the "bridegroom," attuned to His miraculous entry.

Or… perhaps, we will be cursing the television set, punching the channel changer and wondering why the power company can't keep the squirrels off the power line.

Reawaken in me, Lord, a sense of wonder and humility. Create in me the desire to seek you, perhaps turning off the lights and standing under the star lit canopy. Call to me early, let me await the painting of your hand on the morning sky. Clear my calendar that I might look for the miraculous in the subtleties of nature and the mix of colors in the hues of your setting sun - Amen.

"Pow, right between the eyes..."
Psalm 141

Let the just strike me; that is kindness;
let them rebuke me; that is oil for my head.
All this I shall not refuse,
but will pray despite these trials.
Psalm 141:5

His friends had all sold him out. They broke their covenant with God, leaving behind the customs and traditions of the Lord. However, instead of receiving the punishment of God, they had become affluent in the world. Occasionally they would remember their old friend from the temple and throw him a bone and some scraps. They offer him jobs and business opportunities if only he would leave behind his 'old ways'. Still, the Psalmist remains true to his beliefs, maintaining the precepts of the Lord, hungering for the knowledge of his God. In fact, he believes, it would be better to be struck and rebuked by a righteous man than to follow the ways of those who had sold out around him. And so, he hangs on…

Is this Psalm pertinent to our generation? Are there temptations and invitations that would pull us away from the values of the Lord? From the love of our family, the needs of the poor, the work of the Lord? Certainly, these are rhetorical questions.

Our values are so very backwards in heavenly terms. One need only view the television set to see the distracting rewards of this world. We pay millions to the contemporary oracles who will help us 'make it' in worldly terms. We pay money to increase our worldly wealth, yet, we do not recognize the eternal investment we can make each moment we stop to pay heed to those in need. We can see the financial advisor in black suit and power tie, but we cannot see the face of Jesus in the child dropping out in eighth grade. The voice and the counsel of Jesus seem mute in comparison. Jesus is there to speak to us daily through acts of love that we can offer to those in need. However, we cannot hear him through the implanted desires given by fancy car salesmen who fill our willing minds with images of prestige - if we would simply purchase the newest luxury sedan. Still, Jesus persistently calls out to us every time we pass by the impoverished on any street corner, in any community in our world.

It may be alien for us to image a person who would seek out a righteous man to strike them with rebuke. Alien for us to imagine that this would be an 'honor' for which we should pray. Yet, it is exactly what most of us need in this materially overwhelmed society. The counsel of 'Make More - Spend More' is overwhelmingly present, like a parasite sucking away at the vitality of our soul. We do not see the gaunt paleness of our inmost being in the face of our overfed physical bodies. We need the counsel of the spiritually wise to command us to "Wake Up." Indeed, to slap our souls into consciousness. To alert us to the love of Jesus that is found at any moment in the needs of those around us.

Our very souls are on the line - as are the souls of our children. Let us pray with the Psalmist; "Lord, re-direct us with the back of your hand. Do not hesitate to give us a firm 'whack' between the eyes to alert us to our dangerous predicament."

Lord, take control of my life this morning. Steer me to the hospital this morning, to the rest home, the school, the jail. Give me an overwhelming need to seek your face in the needs of my community. Amen.

Fruit and Responsibility

Psalm 52

But I, like an olive tree in the house of God,
trust in God's faithful love forever.
Psalm 52:10

I can't think of a more vulnerable position then to be a fruit or nut-bearing tree inside someone's orchard. Your existence depends on your continued ability to bear fruit; your ability to bear fruit depends on your Owner's continued care and knowledge. We've already seen how Jesus treated the fig tree that was given a prime position and did not bear fruit. One touch and it was gone. As William Barclay (the famed Scottish theologian) would often say that our place as Christians is not a "privilege, but a responsibility."

Simultaneously, we can trust that He - who planted us in the precious space of His courtyard - did so because he greatly desired that we would bear fruit. He has great skill and knowledge and wants nothing more than to see us bloom. God will go - and has gone - to great lengths to see that each of us blooms.

However, what is the fruit that the Lord expects of us?

All of scripture points to God's desire for us to know true joy. We find that joy in praising Him, rejoicing in His creation and in caring for His people. Paul tells us the fruits of the Spirit that God desires to see grow in us in Galatians 5:22-23, "The fruit of the Spirit is love, joy, peace, patience, kindness, generosity, faithfulness, gentleness, self-control."

We've been given a prized position in God's orchard. With that gift comes expectations, responsibilities. We must produce the fruit of the Spirit in our life bringing praise to our Creator and joy to our relationship.

Send us your Spirit, Lord. Let us bask in her presence like a tree in the warm sunshine. Nurture us with your care, Lord. Help us grow deep and strong and bear fruit that will please you - Amen.

"Base"
Psalm 91

You who dwell in the shelter of the Most High,
who abide in the shadow of the Almighty,
Say to the LORD, "My refuge and fortress,
my God in whom I trust."
Psalm 91:1-2

I am so blessed. Part of my job allows me to do wonderful things like play tag with children. It's even in my job description: 'Other things as needed'. After all, what's more needed in this world than a good game of tag?

Not being as 'spry' as I was twenty years ago, I usually just play 'base'. It is a tricky position allowing me the chance to get hugs as part of my 'other things as needed' assignment. On a good day, I might get as many as 60 hugs: 40 with the little ones and another 20 at a place to be disclosed later.

I love being base. Children run to me worked up with fear. When they grab my leg or waste, I get to roar like a protecting lion. Then, I get a huge hug (sometimes even a peck on the cheek). I was the great defender, I wrapped them in the shield of my wings, I dismissed their fears with a roar that arose from the bottom of my lungs. How's that for perks and benefits of the workplace? Now, keep in mind: "I get paid for this!"

Now, about those other twenty hugs? Late afternoons often find me swinging by a nursing home. There, I play 'base' as well. The only difference is that I go room to room instead of waiting for the hugs to come to me. I still bring a hug and deal with fears and bring protection from monsters of the grown-up sort. I guess I am sort like; 'Heals on Wheels'.

However, in both situations, I must admit it is the guy playing 'base' that gets the most out of the game. I am rich with hugs, rich with smiles and rich with thanksgiving. Still, I've learned that you don't have to do this for a living - you could also do this work just to become more alive. The job requirements read: Wanted, one warm face ready to smile, listen, sometimes 'roar' and a disposition for hugging. Need not apply, just show regularly up at your local nursing home or school.

Help me be that warm body, Lord. Too often, too easily we become cold long before our time. Heat me up Lord, with a smile, with hugs, with praise and laughter. Heat my life up with prayers of love and acts of service - Amen.

The peaceful sleep of a restless father
Psalm 4

In peace I shall both lie down and sleep,
for you alone, LORD, make me secure.
Psalm 4:9

There are few things that keep me awake at night more than the coughs of a sick child. As an infant, my daughter would often fight bouts of pneumonia. At those times, there was no personal pain or sickness that I would not personally bear rather than helplessly observe my baby as she fought that viral battle. I would hold her, with tears in my eyes, as her lethargic body waged the inner war against a potentially fatal virus. My prayers were never so fierce, nor my thanksgiving so ardent as when she would slowly return to wellness, the fever breaking, the color flushing her face again, her pupils focusing on those around her.

Then, only, would I finally collapse with relief. Finally, I would sleep soundly.

Fear is often a companion of faith. Like object and shadow, one mimics the other's reality. The real key in life is to discern which reality exists. Personally, I do not choose the reality of fear; I believe it is but a shadow of truth. I believe that truth is faith and faith is light to a shadowed world. It is faith that gives me hope in the face of fear. It reminds me of one greater than myself; the Healer of all - the One who brings peace to a frightened father. I trust in the purpose of life and find hope in the eternal wisdom of a loving God who rules - not in chaos - but through cosmos, order.

Faith brings peace to this father's sleep. Even though my imperfect faith is like a rugged landscape that rises at times to incredible heights then, suddenly plummets to despairing depths. Still, there is - at the core - a sense of hope and trust. For I believe my child is in the hands of One who is greater, wiser and kinder than any worldly healer can offer. That alone is what brings peaceful rest to a sometimes frightened father.

Lord, all peace is passing except that found in you. All too often, I try to build my peace upon things collected, earthly things both trivial and temporal in your sight. Let me drink deeply from the source of peace. Let me embrace fully your words of hope and healing. Let me find, in you, my truest fulfillment. - Amen

The House of the Heart

Psalm 26

LORD, I love the house where you dwell,
the tenting-place of your glory.
Psalm 26:8

I caught myself becoming a Pharisee the other day. I had taken my children to the beach and began to build a sandcastle with them. Somewhere, in the first few minutes of building, it went from being "our" project to mine. I found myself giving orders rather than asking for suggestions, saying things like, "don't touch that," and, "be careful, you'll smash that section."

In a fairly short period, I found myself building sandcastles all alone. At that point, I felt pretty darn foolish. Here was this wonderful opportunity to build a family memory; to pile up a little sand together on the beach - sand that was minutes from being washed away. Yet, there I was panicking about this wall or that, shouting: "Don't smash that..."

This is an ugly side of human nature - or, at least my nature as a human. Sometimes, my projects become more important than His people. Rules, policies, books and computers, all became more important than those around me. No wonder God was so hesitant about letting David build a temple to him, "did I ever utter a word to any one of the judges whom I charged to tend my people Israel, to ask: Why have you not built me a house of cedar?'" (2 Samuel 7:7).

God knew about our tendency to worship things and turn from him. He must have known how - over time - worship of the temple would become more important than the God we would attempt to enshrine and the people that he loved.

So, when God's Child came, where did he go? Like his Father, you could find Jesus in the fields, on the lake shores, in the houses and on the roads. Not just because of the splendor of God's creation but, also because that's where he found the simple people of God. He brought a whole new order to worship; He met God on the mountains, in the desert and in gardens. His altar was the lush green hill sides; his podium was often a fishing boat or a tax collector's dinner table.

Where is God's glory? The answer is simple; "Where are His people?" And where, especially are those who with the greatest needs?

Jesus left the temple two thousand years ago. His obligatory return brought him a mockery of a trial and a criminal's death. Sometimes, I wonder if he might not experience the same treatment today. Would we be more able recognize, accept or embrace him today - just because we call ourselves Christian? What if he came back as a Jew?

Without a doubt, Jesus is still is among those with the greatest needs: At the fast food eatery with the single mom trying to make ends meet on minimum wage; In the bus station with a teen runaway; In a crack house with the baby abandoned in filth. If we hope to find God, to rejoice in him, we need to go to these places, to those people. Not to build sand castles, but to build relationships. Not to build temples but to make beds. Not to install a new stained glass window, but to install an oven for cooking warm bread.

Lead me out by your side, Lord. Let me seek to find you in the eyes of children, in feeding the hungry and giving shelter to those in need. Remind me that their hearts are your cathedrals. Those are the places where your heart dwells - Amen.

No more Christmas

Psalm 81

"There must be no foreign god among you;
you must not worship an alien god.
I, the LORD, am your God,
who brought you up from the land of Egypt.
Open wide your mouth that I may fill it."
Psalm 81:10-11

This was a Psalm dedicated to a major Jewish holy day. The reading of this Psalm was supposed to recall the power of God's hand in the life of his people. It was also supposed to remind them of their sole human purpose - that God was to have no rivals in the hearts of His followers.

Sometimes I find myself wishing that the Federal Court system would follow the pattern that it has set for many years. In some secret compartment of my heart, I wish they would officially change the name of Christmas to the Holiday season; to literally take the 'Christ' out of Christmas.

For some, I might sound blasphemous. As if I were denigrating a Holy-Day of the greatest importance. In actuality, that is not my intent at all. Truly, I would like to see a celebration of Christ's birth that honors his name.

What we have is not to his honor. As it stands, the celebrated birthday of Christ has become exactly the opposite of what it should celebrate. Such is often the result when we attempt to force Christian ideals onto others simply because we are the dominant culture. Without the attachment to Christ - the very root of the 'Holy Day' - something goes terribly wrong. It is reduced to its least common denominator, which has sadly become; "Let's spend a thousand dollars dressing up our houses and another couple grand on ridiculous toys."

Wouldn't Mary and Joseph be overwhelmed to see how their cave has been changed into a living room the size of three dwellings in their day? Wouldn't it be great if she could give birth on the designer couch instead of a hay trough? Wouldn't the shepherds be grateful to dry the wet dung on their sandals by a cozy gas fire? In the meantime, their charges could graze peacefully in the neighbors finely landscaped Kentucky Blue Grass. Wouldn't the angels look about the fields and wonder where everyone went?

Most of all, wouldn't the bottom fall out of our faith? How would it affect us to know that the child of God was not born into poverty, but into lush privilege? Would the message of, "I have come to bring Good News to the poor," lose some of its meaning if the Prince of Peace was born in the equivalent of a King's luxuriant mansion? Presents, bows, and multimedia light shows seem to pale in the light of the Gift God gave to the hopeless.

So, sometimes I tamper with giving up Christmas. Sometimes, I think that maybe we should even give up the name Christian. It just doesn't seem to relate to the infant shivering in a cave that did not come to leave his business card or even capture a Hallmark moment. Perhaps this Christmas, just for a moment, my family and I need to spend the afternoon in a drafty barn or the basement of a homeless shelter. Places that would truly remind our Savior of home.

Let me know you Jesus, through more than a snowy nativity set. Let your shepherds find comfort in my house and their charges on my land. After all, you gave it to me for just such a purpose - Amen.

When going to court is a good day
Psalm 84

Better one day in your courts
than a thousand elsewhere.
Better the threshold of the house of my God
than a home in the tents of the wicked.
Psalm 84:11

Let's put the discussion of 'going' to heaven aside and talk about 'being' in heaven. Let's leave behind childish images of heaven as a 'place' and embrace scriptural references of heaven as a 'relationship' - a relationship of purest joy and deepest love in communion with God. Let's put aside misconceptions of eternity as a 'point in the future' and image it as a point where all time focuses in one everlasting 'present'. There, the totality of the past and the breadth of the future combine to make a present filled with hope, joy and understanding.

Only then will we be able to even vaguely comprehend (or, as Paul would say, 'dimly - as in a clouded glass') the expressions of the writer of this Psalm. To understand heaven as a way of living, as a way of relating to God and his creation, and as a way of seeing God in this moment means moving beyond worldly conceptions. That is the only way we can hope to understand the statement; "Better is one day in your courts than thousands elsewhere."

In this Psalm we contemplate how following God's will can even bring heaven to earth (as Jesus tells us in the Lord's Prayer)! The Psalmist describes how wonderful is the indwelling Spirit of God, how he even faints for God's presence. How he has moved to such a state that his heart and even his flesh cry out for nothing but the love of the Living God.

He tells how the man in God's way goes from strength to strength - ever more strengthened in God's dynamic power. The Psalmist's own love has grown so deep that he would rather be the door-servant in God's court than a Ruler in any court of man.

James tells us that; "If we draw near to God, God will draw near to us." The Psalmist promises the same. To those who go to Him and resist evil, will experience His protection, freedom from the pain of sin and will know the indescribable joy of the indescribable God.

For a sun and shield is the LORD God,
bestowing all grace and glory.
The LORD withholds no good thing
from those who walk without reproach.
O LORD of hosts,
happy are those who trust in you! [Psalm 84:12-13]

Unholy Whines
Psalm 100

Enter the temple gates with praise,
its courts with thanksgiving.
Give thanks to God, bless his name;
good indeed is the LORD,
Whose love endures forever,
whose faithfulness lasts through every age.
Psalm 100:4–5

It is not often that I become frustrated with my children, but last night was one of those rare, unfortunate nights. My wife is gone to a convention this entire week - and though she had planned this trip for almost a year - it still happened to land right on the wrong week.

I am currently knee-deep in spearheading a drive to purchase a building for our youth outreaches. This, of course, involves meetings on top of meetings in addition to all the current programs I run daily. All of this is my way of rationalizing to you that; 'Mr. Mom' was not very 'Mom-ly' last night. Somewhere between the kids not liking dinner, whining about homework and not getting a movie, I began to steam. Sometime, within the grandiose theatrics taken to avoid the bathtub, my internal rockets went from smoldering to ignition. Then, my dear one's proceeded to turn the bathroom into a swimming pool, splashing water on the floors setting even the cabinetry awash. At that point, Daddy's cruise missile finally left the base as I stood in the doorway and saw the cat float out of the bathroom in a life jacket.

By the time my children saw my eyes, the message was clear, "Houston, YOU have a problem!"

There are certain pictures of Jesus that I keep in my mind to remind me of his glory: The Sermon on the Mount, the healing of the Paralytic, the Blessing of the Children. Somehow, none of these fit my current demeanor. Perhaps, Jesus in the temple chasing out the merchants might have been a more adequate description. Daddy was feeling less than charitable, instead, daddy must have looked liked the four horsemen come to collect.

My children were introduced to their bedcovers about six-thirty last night. Daddy sat alone in the living room with my lower lip sticking out, reciting my Pity-Prayer, "Nobody loves me…" I dined (somewhat lusciously) on my anger and finally - turning to God in a righteous but pouty-sort-of-prayer. My whiny rambling dealt with not being appreciated, with feeling unrewarded, overwhelmed, overworked and over budget.

Eventually, I made peace with both children before they fell asleep. Yet, there seemed a part of me that was enjoying the 'Whine-tasting' a little too much to let go of it. As a result, I awoke this morning with a mumbled prayer. In exaggerated gestures; I grumpily turning to today's Psalm. The words came forth like blocks of wood against my tin forehead: "Enter God's gates with thanksgiving, and God's courts with praise! Give thanks and bless God's name! For the Lord God is good; God's steadfast love endures forever; God's faithfulness to all generations."

I have to admit, I felt admonished by the Lord. All too often, I am the spoiled child; not my children. I am the whiny child, always asking for a new toy or a 'Happy Meal'. Too many times I come before God with moans of never-ending requests and groans of never-met needs.

And so, this morning's Psalm seemed less a joy and more an admonishment to me. But the beautiful thing about God is that he keeps the door open to all that seek heart-felt forgiveness. My act of praise this morning is going to be very specific and concrete. Perhaps, it will take the form of an omelet breakfast for two little rascals who probably need to be re-affirmed of their Daddy's undying love.

Lord, as always, I come with a request. Please make me more humble, make me desire to praise you all the more. Give me the strength to silence my tendency to whine and empower my desire to sing out your Name in holy praise - Amen.

Somebody start a fire
Psalm 111

Great are the works of the LORD,
to be treasured for all their delights.
Psalm 111:2

One of the biggest perks of a street outreach is the amount of time I get to spend with new Christian's who may never have heard the Good News of Jesus before our time together.

Through their eyes, the joy of his presence and the power of his Spirit are made ever-present to me in a depth I never experienced behind my desk at the church.

To see Christ through their eyes is like preparing for Christmas with an eager young child or grandchild. What a gift it is to share in a child's eagerness for the season of giving, their astonishment at the story of the Christ Child, their longing for the symbols of Christmas. All of it so palpable, so tangible and alive.

The newborn faith of a Christian (especially one whose life has been beset by tragedy, violence and fear) is filled with the same contagious enthusiasm. They hold a readiness to embrace the world again, to take the risk of hope, to climb out of the hole of personal despair and back into the world of the living. It is the new birth of Christmas, an incomparably bright star leading us 'staid believers' out of the darkness. It is the introduction of an infant child who is wailing out his song of arrival in a place that we would least expect a king - let alone 'The King'.

Through the eyes of a new Christian, I must revisit the Word of God as continually inclusive, continually alive. Not as rules for the righteous - but incomparable liberation! Not as a family heirloom to pass on - but the blessing of love's greatest inheritance! Not as words for living - but life itself!

For too many years, my soul was a moldy, old book. I kept it hidden, under a dusty glass in a darkened wing of a locked library. Worship was a ritual parading of the book. Church was where we exchanged the dust from our hidden antechambers. I blew the dust off my ancient relic onto yours and you returned the favor. Like old warriors gathered about an empty fireplace, we rubbed our hands and imagined how the hot coals used to feel. How it was to be warm and filled with hungry vigor when every mountain was a challenge and we actually looked for causes rather than scoffed at them.

Then, God sent me to work with these kids. The one's whom our valley has too often seen as 'the worst of the worst' and 'the least of these'. They came in; tracking dirt into my private, musty old library.

They raised all the dust of my set ways, they knocked over the neat rows of prejudice that I had spent so long categorizing in alphabetical order. They even overturned my sacred stand - breaking open my fragile encasement - forcing me to indignantly bend down and pick up my idolized book.

These children had the nerve to ask me to open it and read from its hallowed pages! As if to put them in line, I read crisply at first, looking for pages that would scold and scald with hot burning tidbits like, "Thou shalt not..." and "Obey your elder's."

But, instead, all I could find were phrases like, "let the little children come to me," and, "unless you become like one of these..." Then, I stumbled on the story of an immigrant child born while fleeing oppression, to impoverished parents, through an unwed, teen-age mother.

Is it any wonder these youth related?

Is it any wonder that I could not?

"Great are the works of the LORD,
to be treasured for all their delights." [Psalm 111:2]

I had pondered his words for years, but not with delight. I had read of his healing, but it had been so long since I sought his touch. I had interpreted his works without allowing him to work in me - indeed - on me. I had led majestic prayers about him but, it had been years since I prayed to him.

Then, into my life and private library came these kids. They broke my fragile glass enshrinement and opened the pages of my heart. The brittle pages didn't open willingly, my leathery binding creaked open only with great resistance, but they would have none of it. They demanded answers: "Who was this child? Why would God send one so vulnerable? Where is he now?"

Their fire was so contagious. I no longer rubbed my hands by the empty fireplace and dreamed of warm days gone by. I rarely have time to stop and notice if I am cold. The heat I was seeking now burns as a flame within me. The delight that would make the words come to life came to life in me.

Look around you. Are you sharing dust with the musty books of other aged knights? Rubbing softened and crooked hands together, recanting how it used to be before the fire died?

For the sake of your soul, walk out of the musty old library. Bend an ear to the still air out on the cold street. If you're really listening, the slightest breeze might still bring to you the distant sound of an immigrant infant, born in a place where we wouldn't even let our domestic pets sleep.

Then run. For the sake of your eternal life, run! Run toward the cries of the infant and the lullaby of his frightened mother. Like the shepherds of old, head straight for the manger. Look to the most culturally unlikely place, with the most culturally unlikely people, and you will still find him.

Then, ponder again the works of the Lord, ponder them in delight and you will know the greatness of God.

Break our glass-enshrined hearts, Oh Lord. Flow into us with your most holy presence. Lead us to the place where miracles still happen. Instead of making the annual trek to the mall this year, lead me to the manger. Haunt me with this question: "Where would a teen-age mother, unwed, immigrant and afraid, go for comfort in my community?" Let me to seek her out, and to see Christmas in the light of her child - Amen.

The Only Good Word

Psalm 42

As the deer longs for streams of water,
so my soul longs for you, O God.
My being thirsts for God, the living God.
When can I go and see the face of God?
Psalm 42:2-3

I was called to Helen's bedside by an elderly parishioner who had just been to visit her. Helen wanted to die - it was that simple.

When I went to visit her in the nursing home, it was very difficult for me to be an encouragement. She had advanced arthritis and her joints were like knotted tree limbs. She was horribly bent by osteoporosis and even laying down caused her excruciating pain. Weeks before, she had fallen and torn the cartilage in her knee but the doctors were nervous about operating because of her fragile condition. When she slept, the pain medicine gave her horrible nightmares and yet, she was still fairly alert when I came in. She lay panting, sitting in a semi-reclined position, facing a blank wall decorated only by a slowly ticking clock.

When she finally spoke to me, all her raspy voice could manage was, "All day long, I watch that clock turn and wish I would just finally die."

For me to tell her that everything was going to be okay would be a lie. So I would just sit and read scriptures to her, holding her hand when her breathing became especially difficult.

Only God's word provided a conversational path which Helen and I could venture down without seeming trite or 'Pollyanish'. As I turned through scripture, I came to this Psalm. "As the deer pants for streams of water, so my soul pants for you, O God. My soul thirsts for the living God. Where can I go and meet with God?"

In these words of David, questions are asked by a soul in the darkest pain. Relief is sought; the power of God is called upon for any possible hope. Though, David receives no immediate answer to his plea, it is lifted up in a framework of trust and expectation. Truly, that was the only realistic response worthy of sharing with Helen.

Later on, I asked the nurses to take the clock down and find a picture for her to look at instead. I dug up a tape recorder and a set of New Testament tapes so she could listen to them. Still, I will never forget her panting for breath, my frustration with being unable to soothe her pain, and my need to find some simple words of comfort. Because we are human, we all will know suffering. However, because we know God, we all can choose hope.

Help me be a well of your living water to those who thirst for hope. Help me be manna in the wilderness, food to those starving for a word of encouragement, a sense of vision or direction - Amen.

Tuning in every morning
Psalm 5

at dawn you will hear my cry;
at dawn I will plead before you and wait.
Psalm 5:4

Last year I had the dubious opportunity of moving from one side of the nation to the other - from Florida to the State of Washington. A move is a move (something everyone but the moving company hates) but a move across the entire country is especially tedious. This was further complicated by the solo trek that I made by moving van.

Paying for the move myself, I went in typical fashion for the cheapest deal. Through research, I stumbled on a company that rented vans for a low cost with unlimited miles. Unfortunately, it also meant that I had to do with a few less amenities on the trip. One of those "fewer amenities" was a radio that only seemed to work when the van was directly underneath a sending beacon. The moment I was fifty feet away from the radio tower, I'd receive only static.

As a result, I got into the habit of adjusting the tuning knob every time I came near a big city. Upon the completion of my trip, it occurred to me how very like this was to the historic journey of the Jewish and the early Christian people.

Abraham's little band wandered for years in the wilderness. Jesus was an itinerant teacher who told his followers that, "foxes have their holes, but the Son of Man has no place to lay His head". We have always been a wondering people, a tent people and a people on the move. As such, we've always had to "tune in" to God from ever-changing locations.

These days, most of us have planted at least some roots. We no longer feel like we need to foster the habit of tuning into God everyday. Instead, we expect to find God present every time we go to visit Him in his gilded sanctuary with cushioned pews.

It would be much better for us to look at prayer as though it required constant tuning. As if we were boats at sea or moving vans with poor reception. We need to constantly adjust our antennae to God's presence.

This constant adjustment can be likened to the habit of Morning Prayer, the habit of 'tuning in'. I 'tune in' every morning by waking early enough to find quiet before the rest of my family rises. I pray through the scriptures - sometimes reading only one verse for a whole week. As I 'pray' through God's Word, I often feel flooded by his overwhelming presence. Almost as though I am trying to quench my little thirst from the massive flume of a dam. Then I write. Following that, I block out solo prayer time by walking to and from work (six miles). This combines two of my most critical habits (exercise and prayer) into an awesome morning of spiritual tuning and power that still gets me to work by eight o' clock every morning.

However you tune in - do it habitually. You will find that God speaks deeper through our habits, not in 'off the cuff' sermonettes. You cannot hurry intimacy in any relationship, but especially in this relationship. Turn on, tune in, take time...

Help us build the habit of prayer in our lives, Lord. Build in us such a significant desire for you that we long to tune into your waves each morning. - Amen

Prayer of the P.O.W.

Psalm 61

From the brink of Sheol I call;
my heart grows faint.
Raise me up, set me on a rock,
                    Psalm 61:3

It is believed that this Psalm was the work of a man who was a prisoner of war. He was distant from Jerusalem, praying for the King, fighting despair and pleading with God to set him free.

In the dreaded Ho Lou POW prison in Vietnam, American soldiers were not allowed reading material - especially religious material. One Christmas, the camp commander decided to allow the prisoners to have one bible passed from cell to cell on that night.

Immediately, the soldiers took the bible and set to work. Using charcoal and toilet paper, each soldier copied down their favorite reading. Thereafter they would secretly pass the papers from cell to cell until the end of their confinement.

It is hard to imagine spending over seven years in such a pit of despair. It is extremely difficult for me to imagine being unable to study books - in particular - the bible. It is hard for me to imagine which single piece of scripture I would cling to if I only had the bible overnight.

As I contemplate this, I felt substantial sorrow for the lost years of those Prisoners of War. I also cannot help but pray for those who continue to experience such barbarism in political prisons throughout the world. Yet, I marvel at the will possessed by some of these people to continue with their beliefs, to hold on to hope and cling to faith. Finally, I find myself asking direction, seeking actions that would help relieve the many who suffer horrible political imprisonment today.

In the Psalm for this day, the soldiers pray to be; "Led to the rock that is higher than I." He desires a vista of his home, the peace of God's vision.

To these men, their vista, their rock, was scripture.

The cruelty we breed is overwhelming Lord. Addressing it without your vista - your sight - or conquering it without your hope - your steadfast love - would be impossible. Bring us your sight, your vision and your fulfilling love that we might know what to do and have the courage to do it - Amen.

Unless...

Psalm 56

when I am afraid,
in you I place my trust.
God, I praise your promise;
in you I trust, I do not fear.
What can mere flesh do to me?
Psalm 56:4-5

Most psychologists would agree that the framework by which we view and relate to the world is established in our first few months of life. It is formed by the consistency of care we receive, in how caregivers either respond or ignore our cries for help. Through these acts of consistency, our framework for the world and how we perceive it is laid into cement.

Dormant in these critical years is the foundation for whether we will be cynics or optimists, whether we will deal with the world from a basic premise of trust, or turn from the world with a view of distrust and pessimism. Thereafter, we spend the rest of our lives finding experiences to justify our basic outlook on life.

But, there are also those who believe that we are not locked in. That - under certain conditions and with the right assistance - people can change. Yet, even the greatest optimists would agree that we are stuck within our frameworks "unless..."

In other words, people may be doomed to a life of distrust and anger "unless..."

After years of work with street youth, in jails and in prisons, I firmly believe that humans have a natural inclination towards hope. A "Spirit-Calling" placed by our Creator that makes us desire a world of direction and order, of purpose and even hope. The major factors of the big "Unless" are that change takes a solid dose of unconditional love and it must be reciprocated by the desire to change; to become like the model in a caring relationship. Simply stated - it takes someone who is willing to love me consistently and unconditionally. This is the recipe for change, the tools of change.

God knew this when He sent us His son as a living model of the power of love. Daily, throughout this world, people have used His example, and been empowered by His Holy Spirit, to offer this same unconditional, non-reciprocal love towards others. It is a love that is consistently and repeatedly offered; a love that shatters the negative framework (paradigm) of the receiver, beyond their comprehension, contradicting their belief. It is a love that flows over the dam which would block the reality of God's purposeful and trustworthy hope. It simply overwhelms the parapets of cynicism and protection, the castle keep of pain and fear.

Through this love, the mud of hatred which has cloaked our lives, clouded our vision, weighed us down finally begins to crack. Piece by piece love is revealed with a longing for a new way to live, a new way to view the world, trust is born again.

"Unless", is a powerful word to those redeemed by Christ. It doesn't imply ease or casual involvement. It implies hope in the face of desperation. The miraculous 'unless' is harmonizes with closeness to our Creator. The closer we get to God, the more hope grows; risk becomes hope and hope becomes trust.

Our role is simply to let Christ's love and hope flow through us to others. Let His consistency shine from our faces and through our actions. Through His strength, our lives can become the 'unless' to those trapped in a cycle of distrust and fear.

Help me be the "Unless" to another. Help my hope and trust in you. Create in me the desire to provide the unconditional "Yes" to my small and desperate world - Amen.

Home Run
Psalm 35

My very bones shall say,
"O LORD, who is like you,
Who rescue the afflicted from the powerful,
the afflicted and needy from the despoiler?"
Psalm 35:10

It seems like most Little League coaches must balance the delicate subject of having their own child or children on their team. Like many of those coaches, my son was also one of my players. He was one of the youngest on the team and therefore, smaller and less developed than most of the other kids. Sometimes this was hard for him. He couldn't throw as hard, hit as far, run as fast or chew as big a wad of gum as most of the other boys. Still, what he lacked for in size, he made up for in heart and it became obvious that I had to continually affirm him for this or he would get disappointed.

It is difficult to tell a seven-year-old boy that it's not the "tangible" results of baseball that makes his daddy proud. It's hard for him to understand that the hitting, catching and throwing aspects - which make everyone cheer so loudly - mattered less to his daddy then his effort, his persistence and his team support.

I soon found that my most important task - as a coach or as a dad - was telling my son how much he impressed me when he cheered for Jimmy, helped Randy get on the catcher's gear, or patted David's back after a strike out.

Very few kids will ever make the professional ranks of sports, but every single one of them will be called on - throughout their life - to be supportive of others and to work as a team. Twenty years from now, it seems highly unlikely that our children will be asked about the home run they hit when they were in PeeWee League. But... every one of our children will be asked to develop supporting relationships and make the world a better place to live.

In today's Psalm, we learn what our Heavenly Father desires to affirm in our lives. And, guess what... It's not our batting average or pitching speed that makes Him proud. Neither is it our gross income or net worth. Instead he states: "...you rescue the poor from those too strong for them, the poor and needy from those who rob them."

What is it that gives God joy when He looks at out short lives? Did you turn to me in your weakness? Did you help the poor? Did you feed the hungry? Did you clothe the naked? Have you given heart to the hopeless, brought love to the lonely, or shared His peace with the suffering?

God keeps a very different score card than we do. While were watching the ROI (return on investment) and the RBI (runs batted in), he's watching the THB (the Times our Heart Broke for the 'least of these').

Lord, help me learn to keep score like you do. To rejoice in a hungry child being fed, a lonely widow being comforted, a homeless family being sheltered. Help me reset the scoreboard of my life to reflect your values (perhaps less tangible) but certainly more permanent - Amen.

A Psalm written by Eeyore
Psalm 77

I will remember the deeds of the LORD;
yes, your wonders of old I will remember.
I will recite all your works;
your exploits I will tell.
Psalm 77:12-13

What do you do when you feel overwhelmed by life? Perhaps you are struggling with what appears to be imminent failure. Maybe, it is a dead or dying relationship. Perhaps you are simply living a life that feels barren and void of meaning - like a forced march through dry fields of unbalanced rock. Each footstep is a major effort; every stride drains you of vigor and strength.

When I feel like this, I get moody, extremely withdrawn and downcast. I internalize each fault, rewinding mistakes over and over in my cerebral videotapes. I blame myself for each mistake and even feel responsible for the faults of those around me. I mope about like E.E. Milne's childish donkey, Eeyore, except that he is cute and I'm, well… I'm just annoying.

This Psalm begins with immense pain, a desert of human depression:
"I cry aloud to God,
    cry to God to hear me.
On the day of my distress I seek the Lord;
    by night my hands are raised unceasingly;
I refuse to be consoled." [vs. 2-3]

Shortly thereafter, however, the Psalmist makes an incredible conscious choice. With great determination, he reverses his thoughts. Like a cowboy physically throwing a calf for branding he changes his direction; "To this I will appeal - the years of the right hand of the Most High."

The Psalmist chooses to remember the mighty works of God - both in his own life and in the history of his people. He continues to write with glorious beauty and remarkable imagery:
The waters saw you, God;
    the waters saw you and lashed about,
    trembled even to their depths.
The clouds poured down their rains;
    the thunderheads rumbled;
    your arrows flashed back and forth.
The thunder of your chariot wheels resounded;
    your lightning lit up the world;
    the earth trembled and quaked.
Through the sea was your path;
    your way, through the mighty waters,
    though your footsteps were unseen. [Vs. 17-20]

It is the choice of the Psalmist to turn his pain into a work of art, a song of radiant praise! Could I do that?

Perhaps I should rephrase that, not as a question, but as a statement; "I must do that!" To say "God works in Joy" is much different than saying; "God works in Happiness." I need - as exemplified by the Psalmist - to seek joy when I am not 'happy'. I need to give my moody ways to God. Even more, I need to choose joy even when I don't feel it - especially when I don't feel it. I need to choose to do God's work, to recall his magnificence, to dwell on his omniscience.

Lord, make me determined to choose you. Make me committed to choose hope. Make me demand that my thoughts seek your wonder. Make me remember to turn to you. Make me yours. - Amen

Nanoseconds
Psalm 27

Wait for the LORD, take courage;
be stouthearted, wait for the LORD.
Psalm 27:14

I am terrible at waiting. I will drive to another store rather than wait in a checkout line - even if it takes me more time to drive than if I had just stood in the original line! At Christmas and on birthdays I don't buy presents until the last minute because I can't wait to give them to the recipient. If I have mail in my box, I can't wait to get home to read it. If I get the paper in the morning I can't wait until I'm inside to read the headline. If there are fresh cookies in the jar, I can't wait until after dinner to try them.

Waiting on the Lord is also difficult for me - especially considering his understanding of time versus mine. To me, a long wait is equal to the amount of time I am forced to read about the starlet who had an alien's baby while the cashier with the overdue break rings up a shopper's thirteenth item in the twelve-item express line. Waiting begins the moment I click on a computer program's icon and lasts until the moment I am happily typing away. It's a "nanosecond" issue...

To God, waiting is measured differently. I recall that forty was a big number for Him. Jesus spent forty days of fasting in the wilderness. Moses spent forty years wandering in the desert. Noah spent forty days in a stifling boat with smelly animals. Yet, I get frustrated by thirty-second commercials. I recall that Abraham was seventy-five when God promised him a son and ninety-nine when God delivered the bundle.

A lot of my waiting phobia correlates with how I fill my down time. Jesus filled it with prayer, I fill it with impatience. He was reverent, I am rushed. Jesus waited in expectation, I wait in frustration.

I fill my months with projects, my weeks with goals, my days with tasks and my moments with stress. I create all of those plots and plans in my grandiose mind. I attach the deadlines; I attribute the mental stress and punishment that compiles as the moments preceding my 'ETA' (Estimated Time of Aggravation) tick down.

Meanwhile, I put God on hold. I tell him I've got calls to take. I've got 'important projects', 'things to accomplish', 'places to be' and 'people to meet'. I treat him like an old high school acquaintance: "We'll have to do lunch... I'll have my people call your... uh, your hmm, call your angels?"

I'm too busy for God?!! I'm asking God to wait?!! I never think of it in those terms, nor place it in that perspective.

Somehow, I have the roles reversed, like the spoiled child who tells mom to hold dinner while he finishes playing his computer game. I've noticed (at least in my house) that mom's do not do too well with that sort of thing. I wonder what makes me presume that God appreciates it any more than she does. If that child (me) has any sense he would immediately head for the dinner table before Ms. Saint Helens loses her cap. If I have any sense, I'll stop asking God to wait and start learning to wait upon Him.

Lord, it feels like a dangerous prayer to ask you to take "my" time. But, then, I've taken and wasted so much of yours. With bold trepidation, I pray; "Take me, Lord." Take my time, take my projects, take my agenda, take my day-timer ('ouch', it hurts to say that...). Write your name on every page, in every hour, under every task. Teach me expectation, patience, reverence for the moments - or even years - that you would have me wait to prepare my heart - Amen.

"Why - - ning"
Psalm 88

But I cry out to you, LORD;
in the morning my prayer comes before you.
Why do you reject me, LORD?
Why hide your face from me?
Psalm 88:14-15

"Why me, Lord?"

So many prayers begin with that statement. It is almost as if we are surprised when life holds adversity in our path. I often think I would like to live a life without complication. I become strangely provoked when a wall lays down before me on the path I have chosen. "Life should revolve around me," I think. "How dare someone else need a wall right where I need a walkway?"

The truth is that the greatest men and women became admired only because of the adversity that they choose to embrace. They purposely placed themselves in front of harm's way and never question 'why' when they experienced great temptation or trials. Jesus was rejected by the Nazarenes, Moses was despised by the Israelites and Martin Luther King, Jr. was threatened by minority and majority alike. Welcome to leadership.

For a long time, Job lived a great life in somewhat of a never, never land with no trials or adversity. Yet, in order for his faith to explode to new levels, he had to walk through the fire. His friends thought they knew 'why' he was suffering, but they only complicated matters by blaming Job. It was one of those moments where a person could glumly state; "If these are friends, who needs enemies?" After their fruitless meandering, Job also began to query God; "Why me, Lord." (You'll see this in the next Psalm too). He didn't doubt there was a God; he just didn't believe God was concerned about him.

Unfortunately, that sums up the beliefs of most of us in our culture. "There is a loving God, but he couldn't love me."

Later, Job would learn that God's love is far greater than we are capable of understanding. Once we embrace that, all of our tribulations seem like a child's nightmare as we awaken to the truth.

Faith is all about trust. Trust grows strongest when we believe during times when there seems no rational 'why' to our circumstances. All the sorrow in our world needs to remind us; once again, that this is not our home. We mustn't attach ourselves to this world, its unanswerable sorrows, its empty promises, its futile 'why's'.

Lord, move my faith beyond, "why me." and into "how may I serve you?"
- Amen.

Sons of evil
Psalm 95

Do not harden your hearts as at Meribah,
as on the day of Massah in the desert.
Psalm 95:8

Meribah and Massah, two unholy places where the Israelites gathered to turn their backs on God. They even threatened the lives of Moses and Aaron going as far as to pick up rocks to stone them. In a face to face confrontation with their leaders, the people denigrated God's appointed ones for rescuing them from slavery! They shouted; "We were better off in our slavery than with you!"

The site of Meribah was named for the bitter attitude displayed by God's people, (Exodus 17:1-7). In like manner, Massah was named for the way all the people (including Moses and Aaron), tested God's claims and purposes (Numbers 20:1-13).

This morning in the jail, Gregory asked for time with me. He was angry at an overwhelming enemy to which he has been enslaved throughout his entire life. He was - quite simply - angry about his anger. His inability to direct his adolescent rage was leading him to alienate (or beat up) everyone who came too close to him. His bunk mate (a man in which God has truly done mighty wonders) tried to suggest that he was at the bottom of a deep hole. "However," he stated, "instead of trying to get out, you would use every rope thrown to you to try to pull others in." I was pretty darned impressed with his analysis - but I could see the adolescent rage flushing Gregory's cheeks. I could see the twin sons of evil - Meribah and Massah - boiling to the surface of his face. Meribah (bitterness) came close to the surface as he visibly showed his anger at the gentle truth his friend shared. Massah (testing) showed in his clenched fists as he questioned his friend's Godly motives.

Yet, to his credit, Gregory 'checked' himself. He held his tongue and swallowed the anger in his bile.

Together, the ministry team is working on other ways for Gregory to deal with his Meribah and Massah. Everyday I learn a little more humility from the men who are struggling with demons I can only imagine. Everyday, my prayers deepen and my respect for them increases. Everyday, I learn that none of us are ever very far away from Meribah and Massah.

God, forgive me, I plead for freedom from the slavery that Meribah and Massah hold on my life. Release me, Lord from the twin masters of a bitter and testing attitude.

Meo-Theism
Psalm 86

Teach me, LORD, your way
that I may walk in your truth,
single-hearted and revering your name.
Psalm 86:11

When I first took the time to really read this verse, I was overwhelmed by its beauty. The simplicity of the request and the hunger of the Psalmist's soul truly reveal why God called David a man after his own heart. I was so overwhelmed with its fullness that it became part of my daily prayer habits (along with Psalm 37:4). Everyday, when I take my walk or go for my swim, I begin with Psalm 86 and end with Psalm 37. In between, I sandwich some hymns and prayers along with petitions. It is a perfect prescription for the stresses of my daily life and focuses me on His Truth. "Teach me your way, O Lord, and I will walk in your truth."

I have also noticed that when I fall away from this habit of prayer a subtle change begins to happen. The change is that I begin to want to walk in my truth, not his. My truth is very concentric and self-centered. When I wander from my Lord, I lose compassion. Rather than growing to include others, it spirals inward toward a smaller and smaller awareness of God's abundance - the cornerstone of my compassion. Instead, my awareness becomes centered in my needs and myself. Into my heart enters the proverbial question of this generation; "What about me."

The further I get from the habit of prayer, the more I get into my own truth and the further I am from the real truth. The Lord's truth simply will not walk comfortably with my 'meo-theistic' beliefs.

Lord, help me resist the pull of the path of least resistance. Pull me towards your path of truth. Walk so closely with me, Lord, that I can feel your shoulder against mine. Let me long for your narrow path.

Promises Broken
Psalm 28

Do not drag me off with the wicked,
with those who do wrong,
Who speak peace to their neighbors
though evil is in their hearts.
Psalm 28:3

His name was David, he was eight years old and he played on my little league team. He missed a lot of practices early in the season until I found out that he would only come on days that the girl next door didn't have softball practices. He borrowed her glove because he didn't have one of his own. When I told him he could use my glove; it was like I had just offered him a box seat at the World Series.

I never met his mom or stepfather. They never came to games. Still, that didn't seem to bother David. Then, toward the end of the season, there was one game where David seemed unable to concentrate. He continually had an eye out on the stands. Finally, I asked him what he was looking for and he told me that his step-dad promised he would come and watch the game.

From that moment on, I had a hard time keeping my eye on the game too.

The stepfather never showed up, but what amazed me was how little disappointment David revealed. I seemed more upset than he was and when I sat down to inquire if he was all right, he simply said; "All right about what?"

"About your step-dad not coming today..." I responded; "Something else must've come up." Silently, I was trying to cover up my personal anger.

"No," said the eight-year-old trooper. "I didn't really expect him to come. He never shows up at anything, anyway."

It was a statement of fact - not sorrow. There were no tears in David's eyes, but I sure had to fight back my own. To this day, the hardest part is remembering David looking at the stands from third base. Though he claimed no expectations were there, I could see his wandering eyes hoping against hope.

Nothing is harder to recapture than trust. That's what sin is; broken trust. And, trust - once broken - always leaves the scar of doubt in its place.

Breach of trust is at the heart of this Psalm. But in David's case it was a trust broken without even a hint of guilt. Pure selfishness broke this trust. My only prayer is that David won't apply that selfishness and broken trust to all his relationships as he grows. I pray that he won't think; 'That's what normal people do." I pray that he will beat the crippling battle of cynicism that he must face.

Clearly, if his stepfather had said nothing, there would have been no expectation. It was the broken promise that created the flicker of hope. Trust is about consistency. Whether I am consistently present or absent, I build an expectation of trust. You begin to trust me to be true or false.

God, help my behavior match my promises. Perhaps one of life's greatest compliments is: "I could always trust him to do what he said he would do."

God, be with David - and all the David's in our world. Help us to create consistency in our relationships, deeds that match faithfully with our words. From now and through always, empower me to be a person who can be trusted with consistent words and actions - Amen.

Those words and that life...

Psalm 76

Who checks the pride of princes,
inspires awe among the kings of earth.
Psalm 76:13

Throughout modern history, the words of Jesus Christ have often been twisted and used to support wars, subjugation, slavery and expansionism. However, his words can only be used to justify actions such as those only if they are lifted out of their original context. Only by cutting Christ's words into half-truths could they ever be used to justify oppression.

In its fullness, the example of Christ's life and undiluted words of his Gospel, point to only one possible treatment of God's children: Justice. He came "bring glad tidings to the poor," "proclaim liberty to captives," "recovery of sight to the blind," and, "let the oppressed go free," (Luke 4:18-19).

Used within their context, the words of Jesus Christ amused the Herod family and troubled the Chief Priests of his day but eventually, they would permeate Rome to its core. Later Christ's words and his life would be used by the likes of Martin Luther King, Jr., Mother Theresa and even Gandhi as a compass point for justice. In the most repressive regimes throughout the world, his words and his life have been used to confront injustice and stand for compassion.

Those words and that life must inevitably turn our hearts towards deep compassion and simple kindness. They must turn us towards acts of giving, empowerment and justice. Those words and that life must lead us to humility before God and service towards his people. Ever-challenging us to find creative ways to be 'Good News' to all who are powerless or oppressed, hungry or thirsty, tired or imprisoned, behind bars of steel or walls of human defeat.

Those words and that life must call us to continuously work towards his kingdom of justice, while resting in his promises of faith.

Your words and your life, Lord Jesus Christ, call me to change. My fears and my lack of faith get in the way. Oh Great King, you have been known to topple regimes and strike dread into the heart of despots. Work your wonders on me, Lord. Throw open the door that prevents me from seeing your vision of justice, break down the walls that keep me from working towards that justice. Strengthen the bonds that will help me find courage in those words and that life - Amen.

Satan's Pleasure and God's Delight

Psalm 85

Love and truth will meet;
justice and peace will kiss.
Truth will spring from the earth;
justice will look down from heaven.
Psalm 85:11-12

I often harshly judge myself by a standard that doesn't seem in line with the love that God holds for me. It rids me of the joy of life and the courage to follow him. It rids me of hope and grinds my spirit to dust. I cannot believe this is the Lord's desire; that I should daily fear to walk with him because of a distressed heart. Indeed, that attitude is more likely the work of Satan's pleasure than God's delight.

This Psalm calls us to remember the fullness of God's love. He heralds a day far beyond truth and judgment; that day will also be a day of mercy and peace.

Two things are required to receive the peace of our Lord:

A longing for mercy; and

The faith to embrace it.

God can give you that faith. Move toward him and He will race towards you. Like the father of the prodigal son. When He sees you kneeling for mercy, He offers the kiss of righteousness and peace. He lifts you up and is overjoyed to dress you in His own robe.

Lord, please give to us a taste of your mercy, that we might be filled with your peace - Amen.

Hesed

Psalm 136

Praise the LORD, who is so good;
God's love endures forever.
Psalm 136:1

As I prayed over this Psalm, I reflected upon the many examples of a parent's love for their child. It can be a boundless love; enduring and compassionate. Yet, I also found myself reflecting on Juan, a young man I recently met.

I've been diligently working to find this young man a treatment program or at least a safe-house besides the juvenile center or our couch. When he 'hangs' with me, he is bright, articulate and humorous. He keeps no secrets from me and (in between trying to be a comedian) he asks quite directly for help.

Currently, Juan has taken up residence in an overpriced, run-down, two-bedroom apartment with his sister and about five to seven other adults (it is hard to keep count of who exactly comes and goes there). There are also a number of children (infants to teenagers) that seem to remotely orbit around the movements of the adults. Juan sleeps on the couch while other people come and go all night. It is a classic drug and gang haven.

One night Juan woke up - about two in the morning - and a gigantic man stood over his couch trying to pull the covers off Juan. The man was huge, he was Anglo, sporting a goatee, and tattooed with a '666' on one arm and the star of Satan on the other. He called Juan by his first name; a name that Juan has never uses (he always goes by his middle name). Juan had never seen the man before and he fled the room to get his sister. Desperately, they tried to get the man out of the house before his sister's boyfriend came home. Both of them knew that the boyfriend would try to kill the man for trespassing.

At first, I thought that my young friend was reciting a dream to me, but eventually his sister called the police and had the man arrested. I verified the story the next day with a friend on the force. He told me that they had never run into this man before. He was not a local man and they delivered him to the county prison. The man was strung out on crack and was, indeed, gargantuan. The officer said that he had never seen a man so large. Regarding the fact that this man knew Juan's real name or targeted Juan's house remains a mystery to all involved.

Juan's father lives in town, but he wants nothing to do with his son. Juan's mother left home when he was four and he has pretty much had to fend for himself since that age. His father is an alcoholic, given to fits of uncontrollable rage in between months of absolute, somber silence.

The first crime Juan committed was during his grade school years. He had been suspended from school and had tried to shoplift some items from a local food market. Since then, Juan has been in detention almost as much as he has been out. His crimes are varied; drugs, fighting, shoplifting, and vandalism.

Juan has not shown up at his last two court dates (the County Seat is forty-five miles from our town and none of his relatives would take Juan there). Consequently, Juan is now a 15-year-old boy, with no prospects of a job, no home, out of school and encumbered by court fines and fees of $20,180 (the $180 is his actual fine for his accumulated shoplifting incidents). If he does not make payments on that amount, he goes right back to detention. The pattern for his life has been to go to detention, get released for two weeks to a month, get high, and get arrested for not making payments on his fines. Unless that cycle is broken, Juan will probably continue this pattern for another three years, until he is 18 and the charges are dropped (provided he does not do anything that leads to charges in an adult court).

This young man has two ways to make money; theft or selling drugs. However, since hanging around our program, he tells me has done neither. I have talked with Juan's parole officer who is willing to stretch the rules a bit if we can get Juan placed in a treatment center. I want nothing more than to find him a safe place, where this young man will be protected, live a drug-free life, and be able to attend school in a physically safe environment.

What amazes me is the level of compassion that Juan has for other troubled kids despite his circumstances - especially his own younger siblings and cousins. He helps me with my after school program; he is like a shadow that follows me constantly. Once, he actually protected me from a kid who was trying to sell drugs on our property whom I threw out (the kid came around behind me with a knife and Juan chased him away).

Juan talks respectfully about people that have tried to help him throughout his life, detention guards, attorneys, and his parole officer. Juan also continues to feel an amazing amount of compassion for his father - although his father does not even want to see his son and will not lift a finger to help him. Certain laws in our State give Juan the right to sue for support from his father - this would also allow Juan to at least receive housing payments towards his living arrangements and medical coupons for emergencies - but despite my continual prodding, Juan will not accept this as a potential solution. He simply refuses to take his father to court.

Juan loves his dad like a maltreated puppy loves his master. I find myself asking, "How could such love endure such harsh and bitter treatment?"

The more I am involved with estranged youth, the more this kind of devotion stuns me. Such unmerited adoration seems the norm from young people like Juan; even though the parent (or both parents) has never responded to them in a positive manner. The need of these children to be loved simply outweighs their anger and feelings of abandonment.

I see this as a sign of the inexhaustible human spirit to choose love; even when there is no rational framework to deserve love. It is undeserved love offered without condition. In my little world, Father's should love their children and desire the best for them. We would expect that in any society. Yet, here is a love that goes far beyond expectations and assumptions. If we stop to ponder this, we will recognize how similar this scenario is to God's unconditional love for a wayward people. In many ways, it is a love akin to this child's devotion; irrational, enduring, unconditional, a love offered without boundaries.

The beautiful reprisal found in this Psalm - "His love endures forever" - was repeated by the congregation after each recitation of a loving God's actions. The words we use, to speak of a 'steadfast' or 'enduring' love are adapted from a single Hebrew word; Hesed. It refers to God's relentless love for a wandering nation of slaves. It also indicates God's incomparable loyalty to his people in the face of their sinfulness; His grace in saving us despite our lack of regard for God or his actions. The farther we wander, the more amazing we find his love, the taller he stands that we might see him, the louder he beckons that we might hear his call.

In my book of wishful fairness, that is the type of love a father should provide his child. Yet, how stunning it is to see this love offered by a child to a father who has never responsibly cared for his own flesh and blood. How incredibly indicative of the boundless, enduring love our heavenly father offers in the face of our own wanderings.

"Hesed": Give thanks to the Lord for he is good. His love endures forever - Amen.

Grouchy bones
Psalm 6

Have pity on me, LORD, for I am weak;
heal me, LORD, for my bones are trembling.
Psalm 6:3

Walking from my bedroom to the living room early yesterday morning became akin to a Marine obstacle course. First of all, it was totally dark, I could not see a thing in my path. Second of all, I was grossly sleep-impaired, stumbling about like a blind and inebriated, one-legged, pirate with his patch on the wrong eye. Had there been light, I probably wouldn't have been able to see anyway - after a hectic week of long hours - my eyes felt like thick leather boot soles.

That's when I stepped on my son's fire truck, jamming my big toe right into the windshield space. I swear the enclosed model Fire Chief bit into me with cannibalistic fervor. Falling forward, I simultaneously hit my head on the rectangular thermostat and landed with the full-force of my right knee on my daughter's jacks. Dragging myself into the kitchen I stood up only to catch the kitchen counter with the backside of my head.

A wise man would have admitted defeat and just stayed right there, or - at most - pulled his beaten body back into bed. But I've never claimed wisdom as one of my spiritual or worldly gifts. Instead, I felt like yelling; "All right Lord, just take me, I won't even put up a fight."

That afternoon, I was still grouchy and limping when I led a prayer service at a local assisted living facility. As we prayed, I looked at those surrounding me. Wilma prayed for her grandchildren who are going through a divorce. Wilma's arthritis is so bad that her fingers look like knotted tree limbs. Mrs. Terrone chimed in with a prayer for all children and protection for their lives in a confused world. Alice asked prayers for a resident who was taken away to the hospital for a stroke. She, herself, was living with the daily pain of osteoporosis and a badly curved spine. We closed our service by singing, "How Great Thou Art," and "Just A Closer Walk With Thee."

I was going to pray for my stubbed toe, my dented knee and my bumped head, but decided (with an aperitif of humiliation) to keep my whining to myself. Instead, I prayed for my weak spirit and asked God that I could someday be as strong as the 'frail women' surrounding me.

When I concentrate on my own pain, I feel only more painful. When I concentrate on my own loneliness, I feel only more alone. Help me, Lord, to concentrate on your compassion - to see with your eyes. Eyes that looked down from the pain of a cross and saw only the needs of a mother and the young man next to her - Amen.

Asleep at the wheel

Psalm 31

Once I said in my anguish,
   "I am shut out from your sight."
Yet you heard my plea,
   when I cried out to you.
      Psalm 31:23

Compare this Psalm to Luke 8:22-25. In that story, Jesus is found riding in one of Peter's boats with all his apostles. The Sea of Galilee was 600 feet below sea level. Over centuries, rivers had cut deep gorges into the valley. Winds followed those rivers down from the mountain and could instantaneously create horrifying storms, usually in the evening hours.

Jesus lay in the bow of the boat sleeping, exhausted from the constant crowd. We can find great comfort by imaging the tired savior; it lets us see a savior who is truly human. Just like you and I, he was exhausted by his day. He desperately needed rest so that he could once again be present to do the work of God. Totally drained, he fell spent in a quieter part of the small boat. There he lay, confident in the crew (his disciples) and confident in his Father.

That is when the storm overtook them and the apostles lost their entire focus. They were overcome by the storm's fury and raced to wake the sleeping savior. I find a subtle consolation that these men, constant partners of Jesus, could lose their faith so quickly. If Jesus loved them deeply - despite their lack of faith - surely, the Lord's mercy will extend even to me in my constant weakness.

My little boat is constantly fighting the battle of faith. I feel almost overwhelmed by the winds of temptation that continuously seem to surround me. Like the apostles, I too, feel despondent and afraid. "Wake up, Lord," I cry, "don't you know that I'm sinking."

But Jesus' gentle response never varies. "Where is your faith?" he still queries. And, lifting his strong arms he calms the world inside me. My greatest storms are always waged internally, in my heart where the winds of doubt and temptation weaken my resolve. That is where I find the Lord manifests his power calming the waters of my soul.

"In my alarm, I said, 'I am cut off from your sight!' Yet you heard my cry for mercy when I called for help."

There may be times when the Lord is cut off from my sight, due to my blindness and my doubt. But, the Psalmist points out (and the apostles later found out on the Sea of Galilee), there are never times that I am too distant for His eyes to see, or too far for His ears to hear.

Still the storms within me, Lord. Fill my heart with your confidence; give me your peace and courage - Amen.

My name is...
Psalm 96

Sing to the LORD a new song;
sing to the LORD, all the earth.
Sing to the LORD, bless his name;
announce his salvation day after day.
Tell God's glory among the nations;
among all peoples, God's marvelous deeds.
For great is the LORD and highly to be praised,
to be feared above all gods.
Psalm 96:1-4

What do I count as a bad day? The lectionary reading this week was the first chapter of Ruth. This young girl is sent away by her family to live in an alien land with people she has never met. That would be hard for me.

Upon arrival, her husband is killed in battle, as is his brother and their father. That would also be difficult for me to handle.

In her devastation, her mother-in-law, Naomi, tells Ruth to leave and return to her homeland. She bitterly is stating; "I have nothing for you but sorrow, leave me to die." Naomi goes so far as to change her own name to 'bitter' (Mara). She does this even though Ruth amazingly swears her life to Naomi. I couldn't imagine swearing my life to someone who has named herself, Bitter.

Despite all these tragedies, Naomi keeps a song in her heart. She believes she is not present by accident, but by providence. Her beautiful song has been recorded throughout the ages, repeated at weddings and on special occasions throughout biblical history.

"Wherever you go, I will go."

A young woman with no earthly hope pledges herself to an old woman who turned away from the hope of her faith. Mara sees the pain of her life and adds it up to bitterness. Ruth sees that problems multiplied by prayer equals promise.

Which song will I sing? The dirge of Mara of the hymn of Ruth?

Let my song be praise in your ear today, Lord. Let me not be named bitterness, Lord - Amen.

God loves... Me?

Psalm 121

God will not allow your foot to slip;
your guardian does not sleep.
Truly, the guardian of Israel
never slumbers nor sleeps.
Psalm 121:3-4

It is not difficult for me to believe that there is a loving God. That belief has never presented me with a faith crisis. My biggest problem is believing that this loving God actually loves me. Without a doubt, I can grasp how he would love my wife, my children, the elderly and the youth with whom I work. I can even comprehend how God could love the worst and most terrible criminals. I understand and believe the words of John, "God is Love."

What I just don't understand are the words: "God loves Jerry."

As David lamented in Psalm 51:5, "My sin is always before me." That is my constant and crippling truth. My sinfulness is continually before me and my fallen nature always evident to me. I am much better at forgiving than being forgiven. I am very good at giving my crippled love but really lousy at being loved.

Unfortunately, a whole love requires both aspects - loving and being loved. Therein lays my predicament. I am comfortable that God forgives 'our' sins, but find it unimaginable that he would forgive mine.

In a strange and roundabout way, that is what this Psalm is all about; "He watches over you when you slumber..."

In my case, this should not be too difficult for God for like many Americans, I do not slumber that much. In fact, many experts are now saying that sleep disorders are the 'en vogue' disease of the consumer set. When I first read this, I was happy to know I was not alone, but unhappy with additional proof regarding my consumerist tendencies. "Great," I thought, "one more example that I am part of a group of blurry-eyed, consumer-prone, insomniacs - pardon me if I do not break out my party hat and celebrate."

Most of my weary compadres, it would seem, are not 'slumber-prone', rather, I would suggest that we are 'stupor-prone'. It's seems much more difficult to ask the question: "Will God watch over me in my 'stupor' - not just my slumber?"

To make matters worse, I think I have spent most of my adult life in a 'stupor'. In my consumerist quest to have more stuff in my pocket and to accumulate the most fluff in my mind, I have fallen face down in worship to the God of the new millennium - anxiety. If I'm not anxious about something - anything - then I must be oblivious to something - anything. I'll be 'blind-sided', taken 'unawares'; the competition will catch me napping.

My god of anxiety doesn't want me to sleep, let alone 'slumber' (to sleep deeply - like an untroubled baby). This god's altar is made up of my fears, my status symbols and my failures. Indeed, if I slumbered - I might awake from my stupor and recognize him for who he is: The one who revels in idols.

I will never be able to slumber until I let go of my God of anxiety. I will not know the complete and quiet rest of Jesus until I let go of my quest for cardiac arrest. Anxiety covers me like a blanket - not the kind one sleeps under - but the kind under which one stumbles blindly from room to room.

I will not be able to slumber until I experience the God of love. Until I accept that Jesus didn't just die for people; he died for me. I have to embrace that my God is not just willing to forgive everyone; he is willing to forgive 'this one'.

That Our Father is my Abba too.

In his forgiveness, I will find rest. In his love, I will find peace. In his care, I will find slumber. But, prior to slumber, I must find a personal God - not just a corporate God. I must be warmed by a personal God who wants to help me shatter the idol of anxiety, to awake from my stupor, to fall into his arms and into a deep and restful slumber.

God, help me accept forgiveness, abandon anxiety and sleep like a baby - Amen.

"Snap, Crackle, Plop"
Psalm 92

It is good to give thanks to the LORD,
to sing praise to your name, Most High,
To proclaim your love in the morning,
your faithfulness in the night,
Psalm 92:2-3

I wouldn't say that most of my mornings begin with a proclamation of God's love. Nor, would I be forthright if I said that my evenings ended in a composition to God's faithfulness.

Most mornings begin like a mutated Rice Krispies commercial as I 'Snap, Crinkle, Plop' my old bones down to the coffee machine.

"Job well done," I think to myself.

If I compared my evenings to another bowl of cereal - it would most likely be the soggy bowl of Cocoa Balls my son left in front of the computer this morning. The only life left in me by that time seems to be the malodorous yogurt-like concoction that has been cultured on top of the bowl after a day of hot sugar milk was allowed to bake in the sun.

I cannot possibly believe that this sight is an honor to God. But, then, neither is it an inspiring sight to my wife and children. The questions this leads me to ask are: "Am I a follower Christ would desire?" Comparatively, "Am I the spouse I would cherish?" "Am I the father I would respect?" You could, of course continue this on: "Am I the employer / employee / neighbor / citizen (and so forth) that I would long for?"

Change is hard. Becoming the follower of Christ that I desire to be is not easy. Sometimes, it can seem so extraordinarily overwhelming.

However, rather than take on the day at one time, I think I will begin simply by focusing on my 'Grand Entrance' and 'Curtain Call' before I work on the middle. I'm not planning cartwheels down the halls to the coffee pot - more so - I will plan to add just a little more strength and quiet joy to each day.

If I can't start with trumpets, maybe I could at least blow a kazoo. This is, after all, the day that the Lord has made.

Lord, my day may not be heralded by horns, but at least I can try to lift my praise above the belches of my 20-year-old coffee pot - Amen.

Blessed Priority
Psalm 40

To do your will is my delight;
my God, your law is in my heart!
Psalm 40:9

When Solomon built the temple to the Lord in 959 BC, the Great Jehovah made this pledge to him: "As to this temple you are building--if you observe my statutes, carry out my ordinances, keep and obey all my commands, I will fulfill toward you the promise I made to your father David. I will dwell in the midst of the Israelites and will not forsake my people Israel" (1st Kings 6:12-13)

The regulations were overwhelming; the codes of the law seemed endless and devoted to minutiae. To follow each code to the letter would be impossible. Therefore, one might think that God was setting up his people to fail. However, even a cursory study of God's Word would quickly reveal this could not be farther from the truth. Jesus, himself, was convicted of breaking the law when his apostles gleaned grain and he healed a crippled man's hand on the Sabbath. When accused by the Pharisee's of desecrating the law he laid forth the true intent of God's pattern for creation by stating, "The Son of Man is Lord of the sabbath." (Matt 12:8)

Consistently, we are reminded that the desire to do God's will is the Blessed Priority. Our desire fulfills and completes the law; it lifts us above the law. The law sets out only the minimum, but our love for God lifts us up to the maximum. (See Romans, Chapter 6, for Paul's explanation of this topic).

God's desire is that our hearts be given to Him, that - with our total will and being - we would long to follow him. Forgiveness is available if our hearts desire to be His alone. David was known as 'a man after God's own heart' (cf. Acts 13:22). Though he sinned many times - and some of these sins were grievous, horrible sins - he longed for God's will in his life. God's covenant is clear: Our Lord will overlook failure if we but desire to follow his will.

Throughout the book of Judges and the book of Kings, one thing is preeminent. Forgiveness was granted for sins if the desire to do God's will was apparent. Still, over and over again, the people of God would first lose their love of him and then fail to follow his regulations. Losing their desire to follow God was their downfall. God will redeem the soul if the desire to serve Him is present.

This entire Psalm lays out David's heart, which God treasured so highly. He desired to do God's will, embedded the Lord's commands within his heart. He waited patiently on the Lord (vs. 1) and proclaimed God's righteousness in assembly (vs. 9). As a result, he was lifted up (vs. 2), given a firm place to stand (vs. 3) and God put a new song on his lips (vs. 3).

When confronted by trials, this is a Psalm to embrace. Feel its rhythm. Sense its truth. Rest in His assurance of forgiveness. Breathe in the peace which is eternally offered to those who desire His will. Wait upon His direction and proclaim His righteousness and God will put a new song in your heart as well.

Lord, give me the courage to be patient, the desire to do your will. Let me hear the rhythms of your new song in my heart - Amen.

Watching, waiting
Psalm 105

He remembers forever his covenant,
the pact imposed for a thousand generations,
Psalm 105:8

I sent Mirabella home yesterday. It truly broke my heart. Of all the girls who need to be in my program, Mirabella needs to be there the most - and I sent her home. I've thought about it all night. Today, I will be waiting by the door and hoping to see her come back.

We have an after-school outreach to troubled children. We have only one parameter for the Principals and the Counselors who select the children they send to us; that those young ones are the kids that will drop out if they don't receive assistance. That gives us a room filled with troubled children. We can only accommodate this because we have a number of dedicated high school age volunteers (many from the Alternative Learning Program). These wonderful volunteers walk minute-by-minute beside the children.

The rules are simple: Respect for self and respect for others.

When respect is broken - swearing at another, fighting, or refusing to help pick up - there is a first warning by their mentor, a second warning by me, and then - if they continue - I send them home.

As Mirabella walked down the block, I watched her all the way until she turned the corner. I wanted so bad to run and get her. Every fiber of my being fought to give her another chance. I wanted to be obliging, to say; "Just don't do it again" (for the fourth time). Yet, I knew that would not work. I knew I had to send her home for her actions, but I couldn't help but feel as if I had somehow failed her.

Now, I am like the Prodigal Father waiting for his child's return. I told her clearly, that I hoped she would come back - but I also told her what behavior was unacceptable and needed to change before she did return.

Now, I'm watching...

This, I suppose, is Unconditional Love. A father, hoping his child returns. It is the toughest work of parenting. I am painfully aware that allowing just any behavior serves to affirm the worst behavior. Painfully, I had clarified right and wrong. I backed up my words with consistent action. Now, I stand at the window - lifting worried eyes up to God. Praying for a lost child's return. Watching, waiting...

This, I suppose, is Covenant Love. Modeling love, clarifying what is desired, yet, not willing to break that covenant even if it means closing the door behind them as they leave. Watching, waiting...

This is a difficult love.

God watched and waited for His people. With enormous anguish, His heart shattered over and over again, He offered real love, unconditional love, covenant love, difficult love.

Over and over again, his people strayed. They left their God for lust, idolatry, money and power. Over and over again we still stray. We leave his blessed presence; we go where Covenanted Love will not allow God to follow. With firm defiance, we look in His face and say, "I'm better off without you."

And so, there He stands; watching, waiting...

As always, I'll be first at the door today. Watching, waiting, praying for her return. I will count every head of every child that has imprinted my heart and I will pray - I will pray that one of them is little Mirabella.

Covenant love is painful. Unconditional love is demanding. How many times, dear Savior, have I left you standing at the door, watching, waiting... - Amen.

All Star Whiners
Psalm 74

Why, God, have you cast us off forever?
Why does your anger burn against the sheep of your pasture?
Psalm 74:1

Last night, I watched a playoff game with some of our local youth. As I watched the players; the most common expression they displayed seemed to be arms extended, palms out, mouth wide open and a look of: "What, Me?!! You're calling that fowl on meeee?!! I'm innocent."

It's funny, but whenever I pull a couple of kids off each other in the after-school program, the first two words I most often hear: "But he…"

Similarly, whenever I encounter a mess at my own home and say, "Let's pick up," I am met by the old familiar standby: "It's not my mess - someone else did it."

From the visual clues and tones of disgust from the basketball player, it seems apparent that Ref's truly are both ignorant and intentionally unfair. It seems as if the Prima Donnas' on the court want to be left to call their own fouls. In like manner, maybe I always pick the wrong kid to have a 'talk with' and it always is the other guy that starts the fight (even the 'other guy' is always blaming the other, 'other guy'). In my own home, I am confronted by the potential reality that the Disney movie Toy Story, may be based on fact. Toys really must have a life of their own and can climb out of their toy boxes by themselves (I have to admit my socks also seem to have a life of their own and choose when they want to get lost).

Psalm 74 is about a people who would have qualified for any contemporary All-Star Whining Team. These people's response to their utter defeat was, "It's God's fault."

In their story we find that the 'enemy' is ransacking their temple. With battle axes, the heathen are tearing the gold off the altar. All things of value are being plundered, including family members and spouses. They are being forced into a single column and being marched out of Jerusalem.

Their pitiful cry goes out to the void of space; "How could you do this to us, God?"

Yet, God's-eye view of the situation is radically different. Time after time, He sent his prophet's to correct the people. Time after time they were rejected, even put to death. The people had chosen the way of the hardened and independent heart. God was now allowing them to experience what little strength they really possessed when left to their own devices. They had chosen sin and he was allowing them to experience the consequences of that choice.

We seem prone to whine over the consequences of our own erroneous actions. We stomp down our feet and throw up our hands up in exaggerated misery. We shake our fist at God when we should actually be using it to pound some sense into our own noggins. We have become quick to blame and slow to accept responsibility. In this attitudinal framework, we delude ourselves. Our delusion prevents us from seeing the consequences of the sins that we choose. Ultimately, God will be the referee who has access to the ultimate playback machine. Perhaps the most courageous step we can take is when we stop pointing fingers at others, and accept the reality of sin in our own life. "Oh my God, I am heartily sorrow for having fouled You."

Lord, that index finger of mine is so quick to point. My fist so easily shakes in anger. My mind is the pole vault champion of jumping to conclusions. Let my fingers be joined in prayer, Lord. Let my fist open into a welcoming hand. Instead of being a champion of blame, Oh Lord, make my heart grateful, humble and liberated from fault-finding - Amen.

Is that a porcupine or my wife?

Psalm 107

Some lived in darkness and gloom,
in prison, bound with chains,
Because they rebelled against God's word,
scorned the counsel of the Most High,
Who humbled their hearts through hardship;
they stumbled with no one to help.
In their distress they cried to the LORD,
who saved them in their peril,
Led them forth from darkness and gloom
and broke their chains asunder.
Let them thank the LORD for such kindness,
such wondrous deeds for mere mortals.
Psalm 107:10-15

There is one sentence my wife cannot stand. Words of terrifying consequence that strike fear deep into my beloved's heart. It is the one phrase that changes her from her normal, loving self into a mass of prickly porcupine quills. That dreaded sentence is: "Honey, I think we may be moving again."

People in ministry usually do not move as much as people in the military, but I am sure my wife wishes that our tent pegs were a stuck little bit deeper and buried a little firmer.

Yet, our history as a Christian people - and far back into our Jewish roots - is a history of mobility. They were a people who were always on the move, an itinerant people, a tent people. Whether following Abraham or Moses, Jesus or Paul, our forebears knew how to stake out a campsite and wear out a good pair of sandals.

There is a historical argument (a weak rationalization according to a certain porcupine-quilled acquaintance of mine) that our greatest trials as people of faith, came when we quit wandering. Whenever we settled in and became too attached to one place or even one building.

Certainly, that was true when the temple priests were so attached to the facility they were leasing from God. In that situation, they failed to recognize the Landlord's own Son, Jesus, in their midst. Instead of dedicating themselves to God, they dedicated themselves to His facility. Instead of making it a refuge of love for God's people; they made it a Bastille of judgment. Instead of marching out to bring in those who were in need, they locked themselves in and those in need out.

Unfortunately, this still seems to be the 'Modus Operandi' in many churches. We are still building churches, which quickly become the object of our worship - instead of a hospital for the Spiritually Wounded. Our churches become Social Clubs, wealthy fortresses to hide in and a castle to protect. In his book, 'The Body', Charles Colson, calls these places; 'Hot Tub Churches'. There, the waters are nice and warm. We sit around in a comfortable environment and socialize. God forbid someone with a skin disease would want to get in with us!

A couple of weeks ago, I was asked to lead a weekend of prayer and reflection for a nearby church that was opening a beautiful, new sanctuary. I took some of my kids with me on the trip. They were at-risk youth who had been active in our espresso stand/small business outreach. Together, with members of that congregation, the youth went through each room of the building discussing how they could be used to provide a ministry to the area people. With the church located right next to a middle school, one of the primary possibilities mentioned was beginning an after-school program for fourth, fifth and sixth grade children. About half of the teens with me that day were involved in a similar outreach that we run for middle school youth.

My message that weekend focused on how the church was at a dangerous point, a critical point of decision. Many people see the completion of a building project as a finish line; a time to 'sit back and sigh'. In reality, it is the starting line. They have framed the house, now they must make it a home.

The first temptation with a new toy, new clothes or a new building is to 'fall back and defend it'. "Don't get it dirty." "Don't get any scratches," and - for Heaven's sake - "Don't let little kids with snacks inside!" This is just about the time that Jesus leaves.

In fact, it is a pretty good barometer for whether the Lord is actually present in your worshipping congregation. If your church is a place where children feel uncomfortable, Jesus would feel uncomfortable there too!
If they are not welcome - neither is he!

Our after-school program began in a church that built a large gathering hall/gymnasium twenty years ago. There are many churches in my community with similar halls. After running our after-school outreach in that hall for a year, our team decided to move. Instead, we were given a little house and believe me, we are cramped. Still, it is much better than the constant nagging we received regarding black shoe marks on the floor and children running in the hallways.

The demographics of my community are extremely clear. This little farming community has gone from ninety-six percent Anglo to eighty-four percent Hispanic in less than ten years. However, the only Hispanics in that church were the kids coming to the at-risk programs that we used to run in the gym. Through constant bickering, continual nagging and even having some of the children shouted down - it was obvious that these young people were not wanted inside the church.

Unfortunately, the median age of the church is over sixty. A large number are over seventy. The gym stands empty except for Sunday morning coffee hour and the yearly Women's Bazaar. Unless there is a radical change in the Church's demographics, it will be on the 'For Sale' block in less than ten years - along with a number of other mainline churches in this community.

Currently, our outreaches to children are housed in four separate sites. As I scan the community for a place to lease or purchase - where I can bring all the programs together - I can't help but wonder what happened to the faith of the people who built that church. Where did they go so awry? What happened that involved them so much in the bricks of a building that they would chase away the one's who could most joyfully fill it's halls with laughter?

This morning's Psalm talks about longing for a home; a 'city where they could settle'. I'm not sure that's a wholesome goal. I would rather have a full tent - which love turns into a home - then a million dollar house that is devoid of love. I would rather have the freedom to follow Jesus - who had 'no place to lay his head' - then, to find myself locked inside a pristine building. I would rather spend nights laughing with his children by a campfire then Sunday morning's listening to local gossip in a plush room at coffee hour.

The house we have been renting was recently put up for sale. In the corner of the garage I noticed a supply of boxes piling up. This is not an easy life for my wife and she continues to be patient. The moves are much harder on her than the children or me. Still, she has an abiding grace, which is far greater than mine. Both of us look longingly towards that 'someday' when we will finally find a 'home where we can settle'. Still, both of us trust that it needs to be in God's time - if ever. In the meantime, the packing tape and the number for U-Haul won't be thrown away.

Living an itinerant life is difficult, Lord. There is a deep desire for us as people to settle. But, it's so easy for us to attach ourselves to buildings and places. We, so readily, become more concerned about carpet stains than people's pains, about scratches on walls, than our Spiritual Call. Take away our security, Lord. Keep us a people on the move, Lord. Don't let us get comfortable with our ways as long as people are in pain outside our walls. Let us remember that your frequent call was, "Come, follow me", not "Lock the Church when you leave" - Amen.

Turn around, upside down and inside out.

Psalm 112

All goes well for those gracious in lending,
who conduct their affairs with justice.
Psalm 112:5

Lending freely is not a practice suggested in most collegiate business curriculums today. Few banks would chisel this vision statement into the marbled entryways of their facilities or run it on the computerized billboards in front of their branch offices. Once again, we are confronted with a code of ethics and promises that swing wildly from the practiced wisdom of our world. Once again, we see that the 'Gospel Imperative' as announced in Isaiah, lived by Jesus and summarized in the Beatitudes is radically different when juxtaposed with the operating manual that we have created for a smooth running world.

Our operating manual focuses on maintaining power and order. God's manual focuses on what is critical in building a just kingdom. The premise of our manual is increasing and protecting what I possess. His focus is on decreasing self to increase his kingdom. His Kingdom does come when his will is done and his will is plainly evident in this section of his operating manual:

"Lavishly they give to the poor;
their prosperity shall endure forever;
their horn shall be exalted in honor. " [Psalm 112:9].

Take the manuals of this world and turn them inside out and upside down. We are called to journey: From taking to giving; from having to being; from the slavery of possessions to the freedom of total trust in him. Our greatest challenge will be to turn and embrace this freedom (this is the root meaning of conversion - Metanoia). To live 'inside out' and 'upside down' in response to God's Good News. Even more, to live in opposition to this world's subtle whispering: "Let me tell you how things really are..." That's the fruit that Satan would have you bite into, that's the operating manual he passed onto us from the very beginning. He doesn't dare say, "God is dead." That would be much too blatant. Instead, he whispers: "God is irrelevant, his manual is nice, but his premise is flawed, it doesn't work. Sure, he made the world, but we gotta run it."

All the things that are most important to happiness are found in giving, in letting go, in 'Dis-Possessing'. All joy - true joy - is based in watching happiness on the face of another person rather than our own. The greatest prize of a stable parent or teacher is seeing a child grasp an important concept; to see her empowered (freed from dependency on us), rather than enabled (hampered by dependency on us).

The sole path to eternal joy, continual joy, even immediate joy is "I must decrease, so he can increase."

Is God relevant? Are his words real? Is he really omnipotent?

If you say, "yes," then you must say it resoundingly. To say it in any other way is to court death. Ask, "What do I need to get rid of today?" "What possession, anger, compulsion or habit is keeping me from living by his manual?" Turn around, upside down, inside out and let go. This is the way to salvation.

Humble me, Lord. Teach me your way. Empty me, Lord. Fill me with your Spirit - Amen.

Which caste was outcast?

Psalm 101

Each morning I clear the wicked from the land,
and rid the LORD'S city of all evildoers.
Psalm 101:8

This verse is dreadfully uncomfortable to me. I spend most of my days working with kids who are trying to get out of gangs, trying to quit drugs, and trying not to get beat up on the streets, the school yards, or at home. The community in which I live thinks of them as 'the wicked ones' - the outcasts mentioned in today's Psalm.

For years, people have created innovative means to attempt to banish them from the city whether it be through zoning, rent increases, noise ordinances, punishing kids as adults or building more jails.

The result has not been less crime, but more; more distrust, increased distance and a seething undercurrent of racism. There has been no peace or resolution through these devices, no comfort and certainly no vision of hope. Only more fear, more alienation. On one side, there are the fears of poverty and fears of the future. On the other side of the situation, there is the fear of being violated or robbed, fear of unsafe neighborhoods, lower property values, or increased taxes, commercial decline and poorer education. And, oddly enough, in our community, all of these fears have been realized by the ill-planned actions of well-meaning people.

There is no pride, peace or joy in this course of action. No hint of heaven or foundation of God.

The Pharisees took the words of the Psalmist literally. The Pharisee's - who's very name meant 'The Separated Ones' - had laws preventing them from associating with the sick, the dead, and the non-believer. Their very lives were based not in what they did, but what they didn't do; with whom they didn't associate. They led lives of perfection but lives without compassion.

This Psalm is uncomfortable to me because I do not see Jesus in its emphasis. I do not see Jesus distancing himself from the impoverished or the suffering; from those sick of body, spirit or mind.

In fact, the Gospel tells us of a Jesus seeking the most tormented, the most powerless of any city, nation, of the world and living among them. In my town, the group that is most alienated would be these 'gang kids'. Jesus would not exclude them; he would run to embrace them.

Ours is the God who embraces sinners. When we finally admit to being lost, sick, hungry, or a sinner - we stand the greatest chance of receiving the blessing of the Son of God. In his town, in his day, tax collectors were among the most despised sinners and the most hated citizens. Yet, rather than becoming a 'Separated One'. Rather than distancing himself from them, Jesus ran to embrace these 'evildoers'. This excerpt (from Luke 5:27-31), clearly teaches us the mindset of Jesus through his physical presence with sinners (the Tax Collectors) and his spiritual distance with the powerful (the Pharisees):

After this he went out and saw a tax collector named Levi sitting at the customs post. He said to him, "Follow me." And leaving everything behind, he got up and followed him. Then Levi gave a great banquet for him in his house, and a large crowd of tax collectors and others were at table with them. The Pharisees and their scribes complained to his disciples, saying, "Why do you eat and drink with tax collectors and sinners?" Jesus said to them in reply, "Those who are healthy do not need a physician, but the sick do. I have not come to call the righteous to repentance but sinners."

Jesus had a way of turning the values of this world backwards and up side right. This morning's Psalm seems out of touch with the Jesus of the New Testament. The message of the Son of God who came for the sinner and the sick seems to be opposite with the Psalmist who writes:

"Each morning I clear the wicked from the land,
 and rid the LORD'S city of all evildoers." (Psalm 101:8)

Yet, there is one potential connection between the life of Jesus and words of this Psalmist. In Matthew 21:12-14, this linking pin becomes apparent as Jesus teaches us the true character of who is 'wicked' and who will be 'cut off' from salvation.

Jesus goes to the temple of Jerusalem - the most holy gathering place of his people. There, he strips off his belt and uses it as a whip to drive out the money changers. He accuses them of making his house into a den of robbers instead of a house of prayer. Immediately after cleansing the temple [in verse 14], the blind and lame begin to come to the temple - to be healed by the Son of God. The children come in and shout, "Hosanna to the Son of David," proclaiming Christ's heritage as God's cherished child. "Praise the Heavenly Prince," they exclaim.

The House of God is suddenly filled with loud children, with the alienated, the sick and the lame and the pockets of Chief Priests and Pharisees lose many for every minute the Son of God holds the money changers at bay. You see, the money changers were granted license by the Chief Priest. They were often relatives and other family members of the temple's ruling class.

So, they are indignant. They want Jesus to silence the children. They want to restore their order (and their income) back to the temple. Jesus quotes Psalm 8:3,

"Out of the mouths of babes and infants
 you have drawn a defense against your foes,
 to silence enemy and avenger."

That night, the weary Son of God goes to the hillside to sleep while the Chief Priests plot to have him killed.

This upside-down, right-side up Gospel, offers us perspective about God's reign of justice versus the world's reign of power. If we read this Psalm through the eyes of a 'Savior of the sick and sinful,' then; "Who are the evil ones that Jesus would drive from the City of God?" "Who is not welcome there?" "Who is to be silenced and cut off?"

The Gospel tells me it was not the children, it was not the powerless and it was not the sick. The Gospel tells me that it was the powerful, the Separated Ones, the rich. Many will find this Gospel uncomfortable - like the money changers feeling the sting of Jesus' belt. But, for the kids I work with, for the one's who live in constant fear and powerlessness - this is Good News. This is a welcome God.

My Lord and God, save me. Save me from being a "Separated One" - a Pharisee - Amen.

In a fly's heartbeat

Psalm 90

Seventy is the sum of our years,
or eighty, if we are strong;
Most of them are sorrow and toil;
they pass quickly, we are all but gone.
Psalm 90:10

I read, in a very reputable journal (while waiting in a local grocery check out line), that every living creature gets a certain number of heartbeats - and that's it. Maybe the number was around 35 to 40 million - but I was wrestling with my change by the time I got to the best part. Now, a tortoise's heart beat is slow, so he sees the sun pass over his shell many times. A fly's heartbeat is fast, so he mustn't squander any of his time among the kitchen sweets.

You and I, well that's a different question. Our hearts beat faster when we are angry or stressed, slower when we are relaxed and at peace.

My first half of allotted heartbeats are already gone and I fear that I have squandered many my most precious heart beats on things that don't matter. They were things that a tortoise (who carries his tabernacle with him) wouldn't consider losing a beat about. I have thrown away my "thu-dumps" on fly matters, fluttering about from sweet to sweet.

I probably have 25 million 'ticks' into my life now - maybe I could stretch out a few more. It is a time when most rational people would begin considering how they will slow down their heartbeats. Yet, I just don't want to waste anymore flittering about for the empty calories of sugar anymore. Ever since Jesus called me to a ministry on the street, I know my heart beat consumption has gone up. I don't necessarily want to conserve those remaining heart beats; but I sure don't want to waste them. I want every beat to coincide with His. Not because I need to be accountable for each contraction (which I may). But, only because I want every contraction to beat with His passion, with His joy.

Make me conscious of my beating heart, oh Lord. Let me feel each squeeze as a reminder of your eternal purpose - Amen.

Living Waters
Psalm 36

For with you is the fountain of life,
and in your light we see light.
Psalm 36:10

We have a Sunday evening service for families in our church. During that time, we play lots of music, but we also do games and communication exercises. Last week the Pastor set up a bible relay where we guessed the book of a bible from letters in a nonsensical sentence and then ran to get another sentence. It was a great deal of fun as participants of all ages raced back and forth from their tables to get the bible verses. However, my favorite part was watching Dr. Dierdorf, at the age of 83, as he raced from his table to pick up a sentence while dressed in his standard, navy blue formal suit and tie. His whole team and, in fact, every table member cheered wildly for him.

For generations people have looked for the fountain of "youth." Instead, they should have been searching for the fountain of "life."

Truly, Dr. Dierdorff is among those in our congregation who has drank from this fountain. There are many elderly friends of the Dierdorff's in our church. Some who are glad we have this family service but would never attend because they do not want to play children's games. Yet, there is also a sad few that believe it is sacrilegious that we have such an event and dare call it worship. Though having never attended, they have formed opinions based in conjecture and locked themselves in with pre-judgments.

These are the ones that I believe need the longest draught from the faucet of life. Unfortunately, it is nearly impossible to tell someone who is dying of thirst that drinking bitter and salty sea water is going to kill them, not quench them. The fountain of the Holy Spirit is often flowing in the bubbling laughter of the little children. New life lies in being inundated by the children's laughter, enveloped by their creativity, absorbed in their exploration.

The fountain of life is not available as a splash bath - it cannot quench you from a distance. It's definitely a "total immersion" type of thing.

We need to learn that youth is not the way you look, it is the way you are. A few people, like Dr. Dierdorff, have found the courage to bathe in the fountain of life. They find these experiences and immerse themselves in them. By staying in touch with children, laughter, and play - they remain open to the messages and movements of life. The universe of Dr. Dierdorff is continuing to expand while for many his age the door slowly creaks closed.

"For with you is the fountain of life, in your light, we see light."

Jesus said, "Come to me as children." He still gives us the fountain of life, but… we must be ready to plunge headlong into the waters.

Lord, remind me today that every time I laugh or play with a child, every time I listen to another with empathy or compassion, every time I earnestly pray for your people - I am drinking from your fountain of life - Amen.

To Make Wide

Psalm 142

Listen to my cry for help,
for I am brought very low.
Rescue me from my pursuers,
for they are too strong for me.
Psalm 142:7

Prison is not a fearful place for most of the youth I see everyday. Most of them feel that prison is more of a bother than a place to fear or even avoid. Some of them actually seek to be imprisoned. For them, it is an alternative to the precarious life they live on the streets. They go in for a few weeks and then they are released to party for awhile. When things get too scary or they get too hungry, they re-offend or don't show up for an appointment with the Parole Officer. Through this process, they can get themselves arrested again and are sent up for another few weeks. While detained, they are protected to some extent. They eat regular meals, go to school and are released with a new badge of honor when they return to their neighborhood.

It is hard for me to fathom desiring imprisonment over freedom. I have some friends who believe that this is proof that we need to make our jails harder on offenders. Take away more privileges, limit activities and access to leisure activities of any kind. I see this as simply missing the point - especially in the face of the youth with whom I work. Everyday, I see youth that actually long for the discipline and rules of confinement. While in detention, it is almost an excuse for the youth to play safely by the rules while others cannot put them down for their actions. They never complain to me about the strict guidelines of Juvie. When they do complain, it is almost solely about the long hours of doing nothing. Those I know who would choose detention prefer it - not because prison is so accommodating - but because their home life is so bad.

Simply stated, they understand that even the worst prison has rules that are more stable and less threatening than the violent life of the street.

In my street work with the kids, they constantly test me for my consistency. They measure me by my physical presence and my fairness. As far as they see, the biggest sign of my faithfulness is if I visit them during their incarceration. Once behind bars, the youth are physically cared for; but they might as well have dropped off the face of the earth when it comes to their 'Homies'. A visit during this time shows I am true to my word - that I am reliable, that I will 'back them up'.

How odd it is to live in a nation where young people actually long to be incarcerated.

For the Israelite, the word for prison - like underworld - was also the term for distress. Both prison and the underworld were seen as narrow and confining. Both places were dreaded, representing not just a loss of freedom, but also a loss of dignity and rights. The street youth I work with do not have fears similar to our Israelite Psalmist. 'Narrow' and 'confining' might actually be desirous to a child whose life has been surrounded by permissiveness, alcohol, drugs and violence.

What this clearly tells me is that prison need not be a physical place. It's more akin to a life filled with fear. It is the fear itself that is narrow and confining. Many people recovering from depression and other mental illnesses can speak eloquently about these feelings. They see their illness as an overwhelming darkness that confines them, steals their energy, narrows their vision or deprives them of relationships and hope. To be imprisoned in a life of fear is what hell - the 'underworld' - truly signifies.

We live in a culture of compulsion. For the many in our country who deal with addiction, there is so many more dealing with compulsions. They are totally overwhelmed by their inability to control their urges and desires. These people are totally overwhelmed by their fears of emptiness and unworthiness. Like the street youth I know, so many of these people are confined by fear, scared of their environment and their inability to control their compulsions. Their fears are so overwhelming or their will power so weak that they similarly seek confinement as a type of freedom. The narrow confine of literalism, conservatism and a legal/spiritual environment which is focused on punitive reactionism seems welcome compared to the confusing world around them.

However, that is not what salvation is all about. The root meaning of salvation is to 'make wide'. It is this that John the Baptist pronounces as he prepares the way for Christ. Salvation is not found in narrowing the path, confining our options, limiting our choices. Salvation is not found in taking away our desires, but rising above them. Not in limiting our craving, but in replacing them with a holy craving. The freedom of Jesus Christ does not make all the drugs in the world magically disappear; but instead, it re-organizes our desires, motivation and hope to rise above the addiction or compulsion.

It is my hope that I can offer a world to these youth that is better than imprisonment. It is my sincere prayer that I can give them the motivation to live a good life, a 'wide-open' life free from deviant behavior, free from the addiction and behaviors of the street. That is the heart of the salvation message. It is the freedom that our compulsive society needs. It is the freedom of salvation. It is the freedom of Jesus Christ.

Lord, set us free. Give us a desire for your salvation that overwhelms our needs for the addiction and compulsions of this world - Amen.

Kingdom Leadership
Psalm 72

For he rescues the poor when they cry out,
the oppressed who have no one to help.
He shows pity to the needy
and the poor and saves the lives of the poor.
From extortion and violence he frees them,
for precious is their blood in his sight.
Psalm 72:12-14

This is known as the Coronation Psalm, heralding the establishment of a new King. In this short, wonderful Psalm, we are given a guideline for leadership as measured by the Lord. Leaders were not to take advantage of their people, their power or their position. Above all else, they were to be committed to protecting the rights of the impoverished and the needy; even to "crush the oppressor" who abuses the 'least of these.' [verse 4].

Leadership was manifested in Jesus Christ who came to proclaim good news to the poor [Luke 4:18] and displayed a model of servant leadership throughout his physical life. Just prior to his crucifixion, knowing that death awaited him shortly, he models a Christian leader's relationship with other's by washing the feet of his disciples [John 13:1-17].

Each of us must understand our role as a Christian leader. Sometimes it is displayed in the awesome responsibility of parenting, in key positions of management and direction, or even simply by being a responsible follower. God's guiding post for kingdom-style leadership was extremely clear. The central question for leadership was; "How will you serve the oppressed?"

Leaders should be evaluated not only for their 'policies', but also with the question: "When was the last time you picked up a hammer, a shovel or a serving spoon to be in relationship with the vulnerable?"

To the God of the Hebrews - leadership was not getting ahead of the people - it was making sure that none of them were left behind!

If necessary, Lord, I ask that you grab me by the scruff of the neck and turn me upside down, that my values focus on the feet of the oppressed. Let me thrill to bending my knee to review a child's discovery or alongside the bed of an elderly person seeking companionship on their last journey. Make my heart a humble refuge for your needy, Oh God, that I might see your glory in knowing they call me 'friend' - Amen.

Even creation trembles

Psalm 114

Tremble, earth, before the Lord,
before the God of Jacob,
Who turned rock into pools of water,
stone into flowing springs.
Psalm 114:7-8

This Psalm recants the miraculous works of God to the chosen people he brought forth from Egyptian bondage. It tells of the mountains trembling, the seas parting and rocks being turned into pools of fresh water. Throughout the Psalms, writers make it very clear that no one should attempt to stand in the way of this mighty God. In addition, it warns that no one - or no thing - had better stand in the way of God's purpose. This Psalm focuses on reiterating a consistent biblical warning. This time, the Psalmist goes as far as to warn the earth and the very law of physics. "Tremble, O earth, at the presence of the Lord..."

In other words; "He who made all things, controls all things."

In Romans 8:38-39, Paul lays forth a similar premise. He states: "For I am convinced that neither death, nor life, nor angels, nor principalities, nor present things, nor future things, nor powers, nor height, nor depth, nor any other creature will be able to separate us from the love of God in Christ Jesus our Lord."

I am blessed with two children who love the stories of the bible. When I ask my five-year-old daughter what she wants me to read at night, it is almost always a story from her picture bible. My wonderful eight-year-old son sleeps with a bible next to his pillow for tangible comfort. In some childlike way, they have turned to this ancient book as they struggle for late night affirmation against bad dreams or even the creaking sounds of an old house.

Throughout history, other people have turned to the bible, the 'Word-Made-Tangible' for help and hope. For thousands of years, they have recounted the songs of the early bards who sang the creation story to a wandering people. They have rested in the poems of the Psalmists who taught the stories of the tribe in words somewhat like these: "He who created all, controls all. He is a present and involved God. All shudder before him, even the mighty universe."

In the same way, followers of Christ have turned to the passionately written letters of Paul. He also writes of a God more powerful than any worldly or unworldly force. There is still joy, comfort and even power to those who cling to the words in this collection of songs, poems, stories and letters.

I have seen the transforming power of these words work for the aged, the sick and the dying. I have witnessed their hope shared in juvenile detention, in jails, in hospitals. I have five youth in my Tuesday bible study that were deeply involved in gangs less than two months ago. Now, instead of carrying a gun or a knife in their pocket for protection, they carry pocket-sized Gideon bibles that they call their; "Swords of Truth."

God's power permeates this world whether or not we are aware of his presence. However, God's power in our lives is not so intrusive. God's power in our lives is cooperative. He sets us free to the extent that we cry out for his intervening hand and fall back on his enervating power.

The bible is more than just a history lesson drawing us to observe God's power in the past. It is a teacher's manual for how we can participate in God's power in the present. It is a 'how to' book for sharing in God's power as we participate in heralding his kingdom. No power is greater than God's. Still, to experience that power personally, we need to plug into its source.

Cleanse me, Oh Lord. That I might be worthy to share your power in a world of powerlessness - Amen.

Age is not a number...
Psalm 71

Now that I am old and gray,
do not forsake me, God,
That I may proclaim your might
to all generations yet to come.
Psalm 71:18

Some people can cram more into a year than other's can cram into a life. People like Mother Theresa, Bob Hope or President Jimmy Carter seemed more alive in their seventies and eighties than most people in their 20's, 30's and 40's.

What is it that adds life to living?

First there is vision. As we age, our vision often becomes immensely short-sighted - not just physically, but spiritually. When we think only of ourselves or just our needs, then our lives become extremely shallow. Instead we need to become concerned about the needs of children in this world, passing on our faith and caring for tomorrow's environment. Otherwise, we become only concerned about my yard, my furniture, and my pew in church. Our vision goes from being 'proactive' and reaching out to being reactive and self-centered.

People who milk life for each drop have a vision that sees far beyond themselves and their immediate world. They see the needs of others and are determined servants. Their vision is focused, but usually on a cause. For Bob Hope, it was American GIs, for Mother Theresa it was the poorest of the poor and for Jimmy Carter it is the issue of homelessness and world peace.

Then, there is mission. An externally focused vision that dares to include the needs of others creates passion. Focused passion is mission. A person with a mission doesn't have time for self-pity. Their days are not wasted on 'who took their parking lot' or 'who is sitting in their pew'. Their sleeves are rolled up too high to get dirty and the stains and tears in the fabric of their life are just sign of compassion to them anyway.

Time is not a factor to them. If they do watch life's clock it is with an eye for how much they have to do. They do not think in terms of how much time until the end, but in terms of creating a more just, more fair and more compassionate world.

Finally, there is action. Fully alive people - at any age - are people of action. The action keeps their minds and bodies alive. They are not only vibrant, but they are infectious to those who carry any sort of flame in their heart. Yet, they are tiring to those whose flame is already dimmed.

My father is like that. Watching him wears me out. A retired professor of environmental science he never turns down an opportunity to speak about conservation and simple solutions to complex environmental problems. Traveling abroad to learn more about life is routine to him, he has studied environmental issues on every continent. His daily regimen always consists of hours of exercise, swimming, walking, stair climbing and weight lifting. And his sense of humor has keenly sharpened over the years. He has become gentler, the gleam in his eye is sharper and the laughter rolls forth with no effort.

I want to be that young when I get that old.

Let my praise become louder, let my laugh become bolder, let my prayer become purer as my time on this world passes by, Lord. Keep me close to you through simplicity, through employing my gifts and fostering my passion, until every fiber of my being is focused on praising you - Amen.

Saving God?

Psalm 132

We have heard of it in Ephrathah;
we have found it in the fields of Jaar.
Psalm 132:6

To the Covenant People, the ark was the symbol of God yet, there were times that it came dangerously close to 'being' God - not just representing him. During the lost years in the wilderness, it was the Ark of the Covenant that brought solace throughout the years of wandering. Later, when David finally established a secure kingdom for the wandering people, they would still take the Ark into battle as a reminder of who stood by their side.

This Psalm tells us about a lost battle, where the competing army hijacked the Ark of the Covenant. The opposition had won the day, but knew that their action would cause the entire Israelite Army to muster around the artifact. They knew the Israelites would pursue them in force to recover the stolen symbol. As a result, they abandoned the ark in the 'Fields of Jaar'. The whole episode wound up being nothing short of a stinging lesson in humility for the great Israelite army of David.

What we tend to forget - and David's people often forgot as well - was that God was not the ark, and neither was he confined to it. The Ark they chased down was a representation of God to the Israelite people and their most prized possession. However, in typically human fashion, the representation of God became the idol of worship. Accordingly, it was difficult to separate recovering the ark from saving God. As the army of David geared up for battle to chase down the golden encasement - there were undoubtedly many who obviously believed they were mounting up to save the Lord. How surprised they must have been to find their inanimate hostage already abandoned in the field!

The lesson should have been obvious; God did not need their protection after all. If God wanted the ark to remain unharmed than He needed no human assistance to accomplish the feat.

Without a doubt, this is what the Nation of Israel needed to remember that day and it is indeed what we need to remember today. God does not need our protection or defense. God cannot be encapsulated in a box, an ark a building, or even a theology. God is neither finite nor fragile. When we feel that God is in need of our protection or that we must ride to his rescue to defend him then we are doing nothing more than illustrating the weaknesses behind our beliefs.

God continually invites his people into the wilderness to remind us that we are to be solely dependent upon him. When my faith is fragile, when doubt is uppermost in my mind, when I am unsure that God is truly greater than my fears that is when I am most like the Israelites. That's when I feel like I must muster my defenses to ride to God's salvation; it is when I try grasping at tangible objects to support the weakness of my faith.

Yet, in the wilderness, God would have me find the ark secure and unharmed. That security is not attributable to my actions but instead, to His greatness. In other words, in the 'Fields of Jaar', the desert or the wilderness, God has one goal; to help me recognize my weakness before him, my reliance on him, my dependence on his salvation. In the desert, God allows me to be 'relieved' of my personal arks; those 'things' that I would clutch and use as replacements for God's unopposed position in my life. My ark, my sign of God's deliverance, might be money, stocks, insurance, my house or car. They become my ark and idol when I believe that they either represent God or that God's love for me is displayed only by the toys He allows me to have. Like a spoiled child at Christmas, I start to believe that the joy of Christmas - the joy in life - is dependent on the amount of possessions in my toy chest.

To dispel this falsehood, God frequently calls me to the wilderness. In the desert, devoid of possessions, he seeks to remind me of my reliance on him.

Chief among my problems is that my response is to look at my calendar and say that I do not have time to journey at God's pace. "The desert is not productive," I state falsely in my mind. As a result, God - because of his immense love for me - often creates circumstances that force me into the desert. These desert experiences are times of fear and doubt where I must question my entire focus in life, the worth of my possessions and the security of my belongings versus my reliance on him.

The result of my desert questioning can be profound. I stumble upon my own ark in the field of Jaar. There, I find God unscathed and fully capable. I am stunned to see how far my faith has strayed; from dependence on him to dependence on frivolous trifles. I am blessed with gratitude to once again realize that I am not my God's protector (the gods of fear, insecurity, materialism), but that I am God's beloved child. I am overwhelmed by the presence of the loving arms that do surround me.

I pray to recognize and hear your call, Lord. Lead me to the wilderness - Amen.

It's all who you know - and you know the King

Psalm 110

The LORD has sworn and will not waver:
"Like Melchizedek you are a priest forever."
At your right hand is the Lord,
who crushes kings on the day of wrath,
Psalm 110:4-5

I looked out on the faces of the congregation that I was asked to address. "How many of you," I asked, "think that violence is out of hand in our community?" Every awake person in the church raised their hand.

"How many of you," I queried again, "would like to see that situation change in the near future?"

Again, every conscious hand was raised.

"How many of you," I finally asked, "will give an hour a week to see it changed?"

One individual raised her hand.

Perhaps I had done a good job talking about the problem, and not a good enough job addressing solutions. Perhaps I hadn't scared the group enough with the statistical evidence of the problems in our nation and our city. Perhaps I scared them too much and they were now in a state of utter hopelessness.

Most likely, what happened with that congregation is what seems to happen everyday in every town across our country. People have the time to complain about a problem, but not enough time to do something about it. We see volunteering as an option - not a duty. We consider tithing our time or money as a personal choice. However, this is not 'God-Thinking'.

'God-Thinking' means that giving is not optional. God requires that we give him our 'First Fruits'* including even our first born. It means that when we open our planner or receive our paycheck that the first meeting we plan and the first check we write goes to His service.

I am not one of those individuals who would suggest to you that giving your time (or money) to God means that He will add hours to your week or money to your wallet. Instead, He will provide you something much more important - a sacrifice worth making and a new order to your life. When you embrace this new order it becomes a far greater gift than money in your account. When we give our life, time and money to God, He is able to shape our desires, reduce our needs and focus our lives on what's eternally important. All of which adds incomparable abundance to our days.

So what has this to do with this Psalm about priesthood?

God calls us to make our first gift of each day a gift to him. The Jewish people even gave back their firstborn son! To give back to God the time or money He has given to us. It is a call of overwhelming responsibility. We will not solve the critical flaws of our communities that create youth violence and gang involvement until we address the issue of social compartmentalization. This compartmentalization has lulled us into segmenting our civic and religious responsibility to various specialized groups in our government. The false belief that: "I do not have to deal with crime; that's why I pay taxes for the police." "I don't have to work with children; that's why I pay taxes toward education." "I don't have to worry about sharing Christ with young people, visiting the imprisoned or the sick, meeting the needs of the impoverished in my community; that's why I put five dollars in the offering plate each week."

In reality, we do not have the option of putting off these responsibilities once we claim the Name of Jesus Christ as our banner. Whereas at one time the royal priesthood was passed through a bloodline; now, we enter into that bloodline in relationship with Jesus. Yet, that bloodline is part of our inheritance only when we do His will. Only when we reach out in mercy to other's as He has done for all of us.

"Who are my mother and brothers?" Jesus asks. "My mother and my brothers are those who hear the word of God and act on it "(Luke 8:21).

Jesus offers this as a stern warning to his earthly mother and brothers upon an occasion when they came to take him home; away from the scrutiny of the Pharisees and Chief Priests. Even his own family seemed to think that his teachings had gone too far. His own family thought he needed to be given a mental respite.

We have become the priesthood. We cannot delegate the tasks of Jesus: feeding, visiting, healing, serving, to anyone. We are called to give money and we are called to give time. In fact, we are called to give everything to build his Kingdom.

And, what can we expect from the gift of this offering? Well, usually one shouldn't expect anything in return when giving a gift. However, the 'ROI' (Return on Investment) of giving our first fruits to the Lord and of being his royal priesthood can be found in these words from Paul: "Tell them to do good, to be rich in good works, to be generous, ready to share, thus accumulating as treasure a good foundation for the future, so as to win the life that is true life." (1st Timothy 6:18-19).

Lord, set our hearts on your abundance. The abundance found in ordering our lives to keep with your commands. Create in us a Spirit of longing, to serve you with our time and money before anything else. Create in us a desire to give you the 'First Fruits' of our harvests. Create in us a yearning to be your priesthood, to wear the title of your Mother or Brother - your family. Create in us a heart that longs to serve your Holy Name - Amen.

* For more information about tithing and the concept of 'First Fruits', read Exodus 22: 29-30, Exodus 23:16, Leviticus 23:9-14, and Leviticus 26.

Machete Man

Psalm 118

*Better to take refuge in the LORD
than to put one's trust in mortals.
Better to take refuge in the LORD
than to put one's trust in princes.*
Psalm 118:8-9

Let's set the scene for this Psalm: King David had just returned from an intense battle, which he nearly lost. He was surrounded on every side and the enemy was as thick as bees. Yet, when all seemed lost, the Lord intervened and helped David break free from the midst of those enemies and subdue them.

When he was nearly doomed and all his allies were gone - it was the Lord who came to his aid and brought him victory.

I sat having a meal at the only restaurant/bar in the Central American village. I was accompanied by three friends and together we were working toward rallying young adults to march with us against drugs. That evening, we were joined by two U.S. journalists who were seeking an interview about our efforts. The scene was charged with electricity. It was the night before our march and an ominous cloud hung about us - an influential Drug Lord lived in a rural palace just outside the town. Many of the local people made their living working his crops or as his security force. Our little group sat huddled around a rectangular wooden table on one side of the dirt floor. Surrounding us were many locals hovering over our shoulders and jostling our backs in an intimidating manner.

The real trouble started when a local reached for a camera belonging to one of the journalists. The journalist was already harried and - like the rest of us - intimidated by the thick and hostile atmosphere. He shoved the arm of the camera enthusiast away and yelled, "leave my '!@#$%*' camera alone." Although he yelled in English, his actions and demeanor was easily interpreted. Immediately, a machete appeared from right next to my head and cut deeply into the table right in front of the journalist's face. There was a rush of angered movement, when - totally out of the blue - my missionary friend on the left leapt to his feet and shouted; "In el nombre del Padre..." (In the name of the Father...) and immediately started the Lord's Prayer.

In the wink of an eye, the atmosphere changed. There we were about thirty men and two women, all standing around a bar, some with machetes drawn and heads bowed. The missionary reached for the hand of the photographer and placed it in the hand of the 'machete man'. They shook and machete man even got to be in some pictures with his friends.

"It is better to take refuge in the Lord than to trust in man, it is better to take refuge in the Lord than to trust in princes."

With no other power to save our hides, I remain impressed with the quick action of my compadre in saying the simple words; "Our Father." In a culture where Catholicism is unequivocally dominant, it would be a fair assumption that almost every one of those men in the bar had stood at the mother's side at some time and recanted those familiar words. Invoking the name of our Lord, in a manner relevant to all present, kept us from what might have been a very tragic conclusion to our mission - and our lives.

Most of the time, my daily resolutions in the face of conflict are not nearly so dramatic. Most of the time, my enemies are the constant wear of trying to please everyone, the continual search for 'more', the frequent interruption of my attempt to run a 'controlled' life. Most of the time, my enemy is the telephone, the television, the unexpected computer crashes, the complexities of life that throw chipped and greasy wrenches into my neat and tidy cubicle. For each of us, whether we relate more to 'Dagwood' or 'Dilbert', our peaceful lives are continually interrupted by... well, by life!

Take refuge. That means to seek safety. Not in the promises of man; this pill, that beverage, the latest weight reduction program, the newest self-help program, the coolest toy, tool or car. Hide instead in the promise of the Father. When the machete of life lands right in front of your face and you know you just don't have the tools or the strength to fight back - take refuge. Seek safety in the name of the Father. Call out his holy name, fall onto the promises of the prayer his son gave to us:

"Our Father, who art in heaven. Hallowed be thy name. Thy kingdom come, thy will be done, on earth as it is in heaven. Give us this day our daily bread. And, forgive us our trespasses as we forgive those who trespass against us. For thine is the Kingdom, the Power and the Glory forever, Amen - - so be it!"

"Padre Neustro…"

Protection AND Prevention
Psalm 134

Come, bless the LORD,
all you servants of the LORD
Who stand in the house of the LORD
through the long hours of night.
Psalm 134:1

Recently, I accompanied a friend of mine - a Sergeant on the local police force - as he did his nightly patrol. I have talked before of the high crime rate in our community and how warm, Friday nights are generally the busiest patrol nights in our town. We raced from call to call while he confronted verbal abuse, two domestic fights, a bar room brawl, a car theft, a couple of gang gatherings at local food spots and one knifing. Every time he left the car, I prayed for his safety and during our start and stop conversations I remembered praying for wholeness of his life.

How difficult it is to place your life on the line every night - in the face of other people's anger - but to continue believing in the goodness of humanity. How difficult it is to see the worst that people are capable of doing and to still have faith in human compassion. How difficult it is to believe that the world continues to have some order when you continually see a world of abuse, disorder and chaos.

These public servants who - while we sleep - protect our streets during the late night hours are not dissimilar to the night watchmen of the temple. Those dedicated few who 'ministered by night in the house of the Lord'. They guard our interests while we rest in comfort and warmth. Their pay is rarely substantial, and there are many times each night that they are placed in dangerous, even life-threatening, situations. We owe them more than our personal gratitude.

However, there are some critical differences between the Israelite ministers of the temple and those who guard the dark streets of our towns and cities. The ministers served one purpose: To bring continual praise to God. At times, they might have mistaken their role, perhaps even envisioning themselves as God's caretakers. Yet, in reality, their sole function was to make sure that God was praised '24/7'. Their goal was to make sure God was worshipped every moment of the day and night.

The men and women who look over our community's at night are specifically employed for our protection, around the clock, around the week. Their goal is to ensure our safety to the best of their ability every moment of the day and night. From praise to protection - that's the critical difference between the people of the Psalms and our guardians of the dark. It is a distinction we need to examine and understand. We would do well to question this constant need for protection at a deeper level.

Within the last few weeks I've known thirteen neighbors who were robbed; all of them within a five-mile radius of our country home. For some of these friends, it was the fifth, even sixth time they were robbed. Many of them were robbed twice within a time span of two to three weeks. The average response time for each crime was about two hours (when we were robbed the response time was 7 ½ hours). Each victim was told that the Sheriff's Department could probably do nothing about the problem. One Sergeant I spoke with said he was finishing his twentieth year on the force and when it's complete, he was going to move his family as far away from here as possible. "Quite honestly," he told me, "this is a very unsafe place to raise a family."

"Duh..."

Our County has the highest crime rate in the State, and our city and surrounding area has twice the amount of crime as any area in our county. People feel angry and abandoned. They feel secluded, invaded and helpless. They feel like isolated sheep stuck in a briar bush, waiting for the wolf to come and eat them. People are angry - rightfully so. They want more protection, many would move if they could. The angrier that people are, the more protection seems to become the primary issue. Along with protection, they want stiffer punishments. Yet, we miss a central question, one that needs to be answered if we are going to answer our problems on a long-term basis. That, of course, is the issue of prevention.

Low crime communities concentrate on three legs of the same stool; protection, punishment and prevention. Only when people begin to ask the core 'quality of life' questions will a sustainable solution take root. We must see crime in relation to other statistics in our county. High rent, low wages, high unemployment, high dropout and suspension rates, low opportunities for involvement and lack of interaction and direction with at-risk youth.

We are a poor community - but worse than that - we are a disorganized community. A huge part of that poverty is a result of spending eighty percent of our County budget on protection and punishment. In addition, our greatest hurdle to wholeness is blame and prejudice.

A couple of weeks ago, I took 14 kids (lieutenant-level gang members), from three separate gangs to an evening worship service in the neighboring County. For four hours another driver and I had effectively shut down three different gangs for one evening in my town. The solution was neither complex nor expensive. Find an alternative that kids will buy into and then; just do it. It cost me gas and ice cream for one evening (the ice cream was optional). Of course, prior to that trip was a lot of work getting to personally know these kids. They had to get to know me well enough to trust that I had their best interest at heart. Still, it certainly didn't feel like work to me; it felt like caring - it even felt like fun.

I am not saying we do not need our night watchers; the unfortunate truth is that we will always need their presence and protection. However, I am saying that we are failing ourselves when we rely on their work by night because we do not do our work by day. This is the work of prevention (which is really the work of relationships). Many of our youth are growing up in an immense moral vacuum. Obviously, their parents are not responding to their need, but neither are our schools, our local governments, our parks and recreation departments or - most obviously - our churches. We can blame all those other entities or we can do something about it. It truly is no more complex that that.

Over the years of doing this work, I have met a lot of people who were great at talking, but had no credibility in my eyes. All talk and no effort; they held a number of opinions on subjects in which they have never been involved.

Fingers of blame point everywhere; but rarely at ourselves. Whenever I am called to work with messed up families, churches or communities, one thing is always clear: Nothing can happen until we quit blaming and start accepting responsibility. We can build the prevention leg of the stool simply by creating relationships; spending time with those who are lonely, high and afraid by day, then release their frustration by night.

Thank God for those who walk the thin, nightly line of defense between us and total chaos. Unfortunately, many cities (like ours) are finding that line is becoming thinner and thinner. We cannot hire enough night watchman. The sole solution involves opening the curtains by day. Throwing God's light into the dark recesses of moral fear. We need to reach out in relationship to those who would otherwise be lost. My county is an example of what happens when people don't respond with compassion and creativity; when, instead, instead choose blaming, prejudice, anger, suspicion, and a lopsided approach to protection and punishment.

If we truly want to fight crime, we must fight poverty - not in lieu of punishment for breaking the law - but prior to offense. We must fight crime by fighting hopelessness. We must fight crime with empowerment. Creative responses that offer meaning and belonging are the best solutions - not the only ones - but the best ones. It needn't take more government dollars to solve this program, it takes time. Volunteering and relationship building are the best, low-cost solutions available. We must work during the day to assist those who guard us during the night.

Action Prayer; drive through your town at night or ride with an officer. Pray for all those who work at night.

Dives: The ignoring sin
Psalm 1

Defend the lowly and fatherless;
render justice to the afflicted and needy.
Rescue the lowly and poor;
deliver them from the hand of the wicked."
Psalm 82:3-4

Way back in sixth grade, we had a boy named David in our class. He had a mental handicap - though not severe enough to keep him out of a mainstream classroom. I can remember feeling sorry for David because of how much he was teased. Yet, being new to the school, I never lifted a finger to help him.

Recently, I preached about the story of the rich man (Dives) and Lazarus (Luke 16:19-31). As I read through the story to refresh myself, I began to wonder what it was that Dives did to Lazarus that deserved eternal punishment. I was looking for an action - aggressive bullying or some sign of physical abuse. However, there just was no indication of such an obvious violation.

In fact, Dives is not shown doing anything that would physically harm Lazarus; no beatings, yelling, or ridicule. He did not curse him or act openly hostile. In fact, he did not 'do' anything - except ignore Lazarus. Diva allowed Lazarus to starve to death on his own doorstep while he had the means to assist him.

In this story, Jesus clarifies a couple of issues.

1 There is a hell - and it is very unpleasant.

2 We will be held accountable - not only for our actions - but also for our inaction.

I was as guilty for ignoring David as the other sixth graders in my class were who horribly teased him. It wasn't what I did; my guilt lay in what I didn't do.

The famed writer and Christian Contemplative, Thomas Merton, once stated that the greatest sin of our time will not be what we do with our resources - but what we allow others to do with them; the silent acquiescence of the use of our tax dollars, the direction of our Government, what corporations do with our stocks, bonds or retirement funds. Merton tells us that we will be held accountable for what is being done in our name, with our vote, with our income and public trust for which we will be held accountable.

All of this was the sin of Dives: To have the means to help, but instead to walk blindly by the needs of those around us.

Thank you, Lord, for reminding me of the sin of Dives. Thank you for this parable and beautiful illustration. Protect me from idleness, from missing the whole truth. Keep me aware that I am responsible for what I do and don't do: Sins of omission and commission. Give me the courage to do what I've avoided in the past - Amen.

Youthful Pride
Psalm 17

You have tested my heart,
searched it in the night.
You have tried me by fire,
but find no malice in me.
My mouth has not transgressed.
Psalm 17:3

At some point in time, many of us find that the paper is a little hard to read unless it is at arms length. We can't remember why we came up the stairs, the spring in our step takes on a slight coating of rust and - even though we can still eat as much as we used to - we don't quite wear it the same way post-digestion.

The cocky confidence that once crowed, "I can do anything I set my mind to," now instead, mumbles something about, "taking it one day at a time." The arrogance of youth looks like a faded prom picture. A photo that you wish had been left at some former residence in a darkened corner of the garage never seeing the light of a spring-cleaning.

"Though you probe my heart and examine me at night, though you test me, you will find nothing. I have resolved that my mouth will not sin."

It was a pretty cocky, self-sure, young David who penned this Psalm. He's on his way to the gates of heaven, gates that he will force open by sheer power of will or with a golden crowbar. He doesn't need any help; he's the perfect man, the wizened one, the alpha and omega of the creation story, superman in a young adult's body.

Stealing Bathsheba, killing Uriah, betrayals by his own children, all of this is way off in his distant future. He cannot foresee the failures that one never forgets; the humbling experiences that scar the conscience and awaken a sense of frailty, a sense of powerlessness. You can't foresee them, but you certainly don't forget them.

With age comes experience, with experience comes a choice. Some choose pessimism, a cynical view of humanity based in a cynical view of self and a sort-of "cosmic laziness." Pessimism is the easy choice, the downhill path. Still, others will choose hope. They reach out for reconciliation; they strive to learn and seek to pass on wisdom becoming humbled servants, mentors and guides. This seasoning brings compassion and its fruit is wisdom.

Aging is hard work. Chief among the most difficult tasks is refusing the temptation of cynicism. If, while your skin wrinkles, your back aches and your bones creak, your heart can begin to soften - then you have reason to rejoice.

Let my heart be softened, oh Lord, with the passing of time. Let my wrinkles be laugh lines, let my sins turn into compassion and my memories into understanding. Let me strive for grace, to be a voice of hope, to sing a lullaby of encouragement with eyes moistened by love - Amen.

One step beyond
Psalm 129

May they be like grass on the rooftops
withered in early growth,
Psalm 129:6

Israel had been overrun by enemies. Now, the fields that the Israelites formerly harvested for themselves were instead being reaped under the whip of their captors. Each step they took must have grated them with anger. The Psalmist talks about how Israel's back was scarred like long furrows driven deeply into the soil.

Palestinian houses had a flat roof made of mud and thatch. A little grass could grow there, but when the scorching Sirocco came (the hot, seasonal, desert winds) that grass would quickly die. This is the secret hope of the Psalmist. Marred by deep ditches of anger and hate, his sole prayer was that their oppressors would wither away and die.

Perhaps what grated most on the Covenant People, was the greeting that their foreign oppressors would bestow upon them at harvest time.

It was customary in those times to greet reapers with a blessing. To hear a blessing roll off the lips of a pagan master would only add insult to injury to an Israelite captive. The enslaved Israelite could only swallow his anger and hope against hope that the oppressor would someday choke on his words and die.

Jesus confronts a similar problem in Matthew 5:38-42. His people are still subject to a conquering foreigner. This time it is Rome. Years have elapsed since the slavery of Babylon, but it's basically the same scenario being played out all over again. Roman soldiers had the right to conscript subjects to carry their packs and equipment for them, they could demand certain possessions, and beat those who did not respond with due respect. However, Jesus suggests a response different than the one found in Psalms. In customary fashion, Jesus suggests a response that is counter-cultural in both his time and ours. Instead of fighting or wishing the enemy would keel over dead, he suggests the radical response of going one step beyond the Roman command.

Is Jesus suggesting that the best approach is merely to become a victim - meekly succumbing to an unsolicited beating? On first glance, this may seem to be the case. Yet, that would be a gross misinterpretation of the words of our Lord. What Jesus is suggesting would actually put the captor at a severe disadvantage.

First, Jesus states, "If someone strikes you on the right cheek, offer them your left cheek as well."

To be struck on the right cheek would mean that the one giving the slap (in this case, a Roman soldier) would be using his right hand. Using the right hand would show the Roman's power and position - his 'upper hand'. It would be a corrective action, a commanding wake-up call. But, offering the left cheek would force the soldier to use his left hand and that would be absolutely forbidden. The left hand would never be used to touch someone's face - except in a brutal beating. The left hand was used for personal cleaning after toiletry - it would never be used for eating, greeting someone, or to correct another.

To offer the left cheek would force the person who was slapping the victim to actually step beyond the ordinary boundaries of what Roman law would allow. Not to correct them, but to actually beat someone. This would be a travesty of the law if done without trial or permission of a higher officer. The soldier might slap the victim to show his power, but offering the left cheek would place him squarely in a compromising position. The soldier would have to back down in the face of the victim in front of all who were watching.

Next, Jesus talks about being sued for a tunic. In other words, let's say you were the victim and the plaintiff has sued you for everything you own - including your tunic. A tunic was a special cloth - sort of an all-weather dress coat. Most of the people in that area and during that time would not own more than one tunic. Jesus is saying that if you are being sued for everything you possess, even down to your outer garment (your tunic), then take the law suit one more giant leap. Give the suing party your cloak as well. The cloak was the inner garment, similar to one's underwear. Wouldn't that make the oppressor look small and ridiculous? "You want everything I own - well, here's my underwear as well."

The victim would now be standing in the wind buck naked, but the person pressing the suit is the one who looks stupid. All compassion would be for the victimized and the plaintiff to save face; he would be forced to make some conciliating gesture. Finally, Jesus speaks about being conscripted by the Roman Army to carry their pack for a mile.

The law of Rome restricted such commonly enforced conscription's to a distance of one league. If a soldier tried to force someone to carry their package further it could result in forty lashes - - for the soldier. In this event, the soldier would start to desperately panic if someone began to carry their bundle beyond the one-league marker. Suddenly, the soldier would go from being the oppressor to being the oppressed; all because the victim walked the extra mile.

In each of the three cases, the one oppressed switches from the power role - to the role of the powerless. In each case, Jesus teaches how to use the power of the proud to change them; how to use their anger, their pride, and their position to turn the situation around. Suddenly, the first becomes last and the last becomes first.

This world is not gentle on the weak - but this is not a message for the timid. This is a message that requires boldness. It was the type of strength Jesus displayed when he bore our sins on the cross, trusting in God's promise of redemption. That was no weak belief; it was a belief that required a rigorous life and a tortuous death. Yet, like the man walking the extra mile, Jesus went to the grave for our sins. Satan scoffed, believing victory was his, playing the high-handed part of the Roman Conscriptor. Confident in his power, leisurely enjoying his pride, Satan smiled wickedly until Jesus suddenly turned around and began to walk one step beyond a league. Down into hell - and then back out again. Satan, the would-be conqueror lost.

Seek the Lord, all you humble of the land, you who do what he commands. Seek righteousness, seek humility. (Zephaniah 2:3)

It's just a pen...

Psalm 135

The idols of the nations are silver and gold,
the work of human hands.
They have mouths but speak not;
they have eyes but see not;
They have ears but hear not;
no breath is in their mouths.
Their makers shall be like them,
all who trust in them.

Psalm 135:15-18

It is not that unusual to see people turn into what they worship. Immediately, I once again consider the Israelites and the calf [Exodus 32] Uzzah and the Ark of the Covenant [II Samuel 6] or, I think of the Israelites and the Temple [Matthew 21:13]. However, we needn't look to historically distant or biblically grandiose examples to diagnose the immediate application of this scripture in our lives. I saw it evidenced when I served a church where the Memorial Hall and its upkeep was more important than the youth who could have been playing inside of it. It would be great to end by pointing fingers at others, unfortunately, this Psalm hits even closer to home - the application applies to my own home life.

Last Christmas, I received a fancy pen as one of my presents. It was polished chrome and had three heads: red, black and a pencil. It was smooth and well-fit to my fingers. It was, indeed, a wonderful writing utensil. It certainly stood out on my person; I sported it neatly in my front pocket. In fact, I began to select shirts that I could wear which would display the pen neatly under my left lapel. This was not a very easy choice when you consider that I spent my days working with kids in weight lifting outreaches, after school programs and selling espresso's to raise money. Usually, I wear a sweat suit or jeans to work. Yet, twinkling from my breast pocket was this fancy, eye-catching pen.

Of course, all the kids wanted to use it. They wanted to touch it and use every one of the three heads; getting their fudge-covered-fingers all over my shiny, new, chrome. That's when I began to notice some less than desirable changes in my own behavior. I didn't want them to touch the pen, twist the cap or smudge the sides. When I resignedly loaned it to them, I would hover over them as if they were totally incompetent or coveting my property. I would over-instruct them as to its simple usage: "Don't click it that hard. If you push down on it like that, you might break the lead. Don't stick it in your mouth! Wash your hands before you handle it."

One child came up and asked if I could help her with her homework - but I couldn't leave to help her until another child gave me my pen back. This never happened with the spare pencil pieces I normally carried around with me. The unfortunate truth was; I was becoming a slave to my pen.

From the day of that ugly revelation forward, the pen has sat at home. Of course, the gleam occasionally catches my eye and I think; "Wow, isn't that a cool writing apparatus. I could really use that, why don't I just take it with me again." Yet, having been seduced once, I am determined to not let it happen again. At home it will stay.

If I can become so limited by the siren call of an ordinary pen, what other things might prevent me from following the path that Jesus would lay out for me; A house, a car, my salary, financial security, a doctrine? Having been so enveloped by a shiny implement, how much more overcome might I be by these grander possessions? How can I prevent such items - trivial when compared with the everlasting joy I can know when my Savior takes possession of my heart and my life?

I am so easily fooled, especially in a world that sugar-coats the God of materialism. Prayer doesn't seem to be enough. God has allowed me to long for prayer deeply and daily still, I must admit that there are many times that I am still simply not involved enough in God to hear his words clearly.

I talk too much, I'm distracted too easily and, I find, that searching the scriptures - by itself - is not enough either. Far too often, I will use the word of God to justify my actions rather than direct me in my path. Even a community of believers is not enough by itself. There have been many times that I allow my community to only hear my side of the story - "Don't you understand the preeminence of this chrome-covered pen?" Too many times my community might also be distracted by the overwhelming god's of their lives - some of my friends actually have pocket protectors with multiple pens (though most of them are in Geeks Anonymous). Too often, we can all be fairweather followers; not committed to confront each other with the painful, but necessary, truth, when someone waivers or seeks 'the easy way out'.

In order to confront the god's of my creation which I must confront daily (the god's of lust, theology, personal and immediate gratification, materialism) I have to be equipped fully by all the combined resources of the triune mentioned above. I need deep, lengthy and intense prayer. I need to go to scripture praying that God's will may be plainly revealed. That I can read his words afresh - like a child - open to wonder and free from personal and cultural prejudices. Then, I need a strong community of accountability. People who are not only willing to seek their own intense relationship with Jesus Christ, but also willing to cross the barriers of niceties and address my wanderings from God's will.

Finally, I need service - to the least of these. It is in service that my most neurotic fetishes are truly revealed. It is in service - especially to the least of these - that my pens are smudged by sticky fingers and stuck in gooey mouths.

Fighting the demons of our day, the god's who would clamber for our subservience are not a trifling matter. We cannot afford to be Weekend Warriors or to give this fight for our soul's second place behind our jobs and our task lists. We must pursue it with unequivocal fervor. As if (and because) our very souls depend upon it.

So search the dark corners of your soul today. See if you have any hidden altars (or chrome pens) to the god's of avarice or vice. Free yourself of these items. There is no greater witness we can provide. No more important gift we can offer to our God, to ourselves, to our families, and to creation. This is what it means to seek God's wisdom at a radical - root - life-forming level.

Happy the man who finds wisdom,
   the man who gains understanding!
For her profit is better than profit in silver,
   and better than gold is her revenue
               [Proverbs 3:13-14]

A runner's valley of death
Psalm 125

Like Mount Zion are they
who trust in the LORD,
unshakable, forever enduring.
Psalm 125:1

Lately, I've begun to feel like Eddie Albert in the old sitcom Green Acres. My wife and I recently rented a house in the country about six miles from town. This was pure bliss for me and one of the primary joys has been the ability to expand my prayer time. My deepest prayers are said while I run on the backcountry road in utter solitude. From our old house, I would always find my prayers cut short as my course would give out before my prayers. Now, I have plenty of distance and time for prayer.

Another unexpected bonus has been how some scriptures and prayers have taken on a whole new depth for me. Like Psalm 23, "Yea, though I pass through the valley of death I will fear no evil..."

When I ran in the city, I didn't pass through the valley of death on my way to work. Now, I do. No one seems to tie up their dogs in the country. On one road alone, I have to pass three big German Shepherds on my left side and two Rottwielors on the right. This is the area I've begun calling the 'Valley of Death'. I think I am the highlight of these dogs day. They give up fighting with each other just long enough to howl at me. It is an interesting feeling to turn the corner on a distant, dusty road and find that, quite suddenly, I am no longer at the top of the food chain.

My wife thinks I should get my hands on some mace. I've been thinking I should get my hands on a tank. However, for now, I seem to be getting along with one simple tactic; Show No Fear. In fact, from the moment I saw the gleaming whites of their drooling fangs, I realized that running would be futile. With each dog possessing twice as many legs and about 16 times as many canine teeth - running fast just didn't even make sense. Aggressive yelling didn't make much sense either - their bite would obviously be significantly worse than my bark. So, instead, I did the irrational thing... I called them. I opened my arms wide, palms up and shouted; "C'mon boy." Not knowing who to talk to or caring what gender they were I bent forwarded and enticed them - "That's a good boy, c'mon."

They didn't exactly wag their tails and bring me my slippers, but they didn't make me a headline in the next day's obituaries either. I don't think they quite knew what to do with me.

They probably thought that chomping into a lunatic would turn them rabid. So, instead they sniffed the air about me and let me pass. They followed me for a little bit, probably because they thought I just hadn't figured out that I was supposed to be terrified. Then, eventually they let me go - I was obviously quite boring.

Since then, I've contemplated running a different route - but I figure that anywhere I go, I'd run into country dogs. By the way, if my experiment fails - and I live - I'll make sure I let you know in an upcoming Psalm. And, by the by the way, don't try this at home; I am an insane professional who may just be experiencing a mid-life crisis. This is my wife's legal advice and expert opinion. She also thinks that my next stunt will be trying to walk on the water in the irrigation ditch instead of using the bridge.

You might have expected this Psalm to relay the tale of a harrowing climb up a high mountain peak or a story of faith that stood against all odds. I am truly sorry if I disappointed you. It just seems that - more often than not - faith is reflected in minor responses to life's smaller challenges; Letting someone go ahead of you in the checkout line, stopping in at the nursing home, psyching out a gang of killer dogs.

Mount Zion is unshakable because its base is so big; it is wider than higher. Often, our faith is so weak because it's higher than wider - built on what I should do, not on what I am doing. It's higher than wider - built on preaching, not on practicing. It's higher than wider, built on concepts, not on concrete actions.

Practicing faith makes it wider. We build faith by simple actions practiced repeatedly; by prayers that encompass a world greater than myself. Through prayers and actions with unsure outcomes, that demand faith. Those prayers result in an unshakable faith as wide and tall as Mount Zion.

Yet, I am also learning that faith grows faster when you're at the bottom of the food chain.; especially, when you're looking up at nothing but teeth.

.

(A Country Runner's Prayer)
"They that hope in the LORD will renew their strength,
    they will soar as with eagles' wings;
They will run and not grow weary,
    walk and not grow faint. "
(and they won't be eaten by big dogs).
[Isaiah 40:31]

Praise can hurt

Psalm 149

For the LORD takes delight in his people,
honors the poor with victory.
Let the faithful rejoice in their glory,
cry out for joy at their banquet,
Psalm 149:4–5

In the midst of praise, God does not want us to forget the double-edged sword. This sword stands for one thing - justice. God is reminding us that he is praised by acts of justice. God seeks to remind us that we were born a sojourning people, one with the migrants in our fields and the refugees turned away. We are strangers in a strange land, saved by the one who was known to his own as a homeless criminal and a dire threat. The same threat exists whenever we fear the prophetic voice of the poor in our world.

God is praised when justice and righteousness are united: When the laws of our land are meted out by fairness, rather than finance; when poverty-stricken children have as much access to healthcare and a meal as the wealthiest among us. God is praised when joy overwhelms His people and they long to be in relationship with those in need. God is praised by acts of mercy - acts without conditions, without pretense, without prejudice.

God is also reminding us that justice - the two-edged sword - must cut both ways. This was undoubtedly meant to remind the Israelite nation that they could not claim God and support oppression. What a pertinent reminder for our day. Too often, we only seek to use the sword of God (His gift, His word, His mercy) to make our claims on His kingdom. We do not want to deal with the side of the sword which cuts towards us; the sharp side of the sword that would condemn our own intolerance, prejudice, or hardened hearts. We do not want to touch the gleaming blade that points toward our own fears festering in the gangrene of greed and avarice.

When we use the sword of God to cut out the personal and corporate vines that hold people in cycles of poverty and injustice - the vines that would seal the doors on any child's dreams, or create a fence to lock people into stereotypes and social despair - then, we are praising God. As painful as the cut feels it brings praise to God. As deep as the wounds go they resemble the hands and feet and the side of the one was pierced for our salvation.

Mercy is a two-edged sword. God is praised when it is wielded to free his people.

Lord, let me not fear to use this sword to cut away the chains that hold me bound: to my prejudice; to oppression; to the famines of my soul which cause the hungers of our world - Amen.

Yes, Jesus loves me

Psalm 104

I will sing to the LORD all my life;
I will sing praise to my God while I live.
May my theme be pleasing to God;
I will rejoice in the LORD.
Psalm 104:33-34

I had a meeting in my house the other day with our Youth Leadership Team. This is a group of young leaders from three different High Schools and our Middle School. Together, we discuss issues of critical importance in our communities. These young people also seek to help as mediators between opposing groups whose hostility may become destructive towards themselves and others. Last week, one of the members of this group helped me negotiate a stand-down between two rival gangs in our town. Though these youth are still in the teens (and one is twelve), they are very active, intelligent and involved.

Last week, we were stuck on an issue that was both divisive and complex. Finally, the group reached a point where we decided silent prayer was appropriate. As we bowed our heads and sat, a little voice from another room quietly sang; "Jesus loves me, this I know, for the bible tells me so. Little ones to him belong, they are weak, but he is strong."

That little song came from the voice of an angel. My five-year-old angel (and daughter), Amanda.

Quietly, we began to hum so as not to embarrass her; "Yes, Jesus loves me. Yes, Jesus loves me. Yes, Jesus loves me. The bible tells me so."

When we lifted our heads, not even our 'hard-core' guys would deny this was a miracle. It was as if God - through the voice of a five-year-old angel - was reminding us of our purpose and His presence.

"I will sing to the Lord all my life, I will sing praise to my God as long as I live. May my meditation be pleasing to him as I rejoice in the Lord."

There are far too many times that I forget to be a pleasing voice to my God. I concentrate on what is wrong, what is falling apart, what is fearful. By concentrating on these things - and giving voice to them - I provide them with terrible access to my heart. Instead, when I feel weakest, I need to turn off my pessimistic mind and shut up my critical mouth. I need to start singing, in my small, croaky way, "Yes, Jesus loves me. Yes, Jesus loves me. Yes, Jesus loves me, the bible tells me so."

Do not let me add to my pessimism by dwelling on negative thoughts - giving voice to words that undermine and tear down. Lord, instead, send your Spirit to me, and please, make haste... Give me an infant's song and a childlike demeanor. Praise you, my Lord, for children who will lead us to you, if we but listen and follow - Amen.

"Out of the mouths of babes and infants
you have drawn a defense against your foes,
to silence enemy and avenger. " - Psalm 8:3.

"Let the children come to me, and do not prevent them; for the kingdom of heaven belongs to such as these" - Matthew 19:14.

Simplicity and Clarity
Psalm 73

But, as for me, I lost my balance;
my feet all but slipped,
Because I was envious of the arrogant
when I saw the prosperity of the wicked.
Psalm 73:2-3

I used to tell my wife that I always wanted to be so successful that I only had to dress up and wear a tie when I wanted to (and I would never want to).

Never in my wildest dreams did I think that God would deliver me that wish by making me a missionary to alienated youth. I always thought that I would have to be rich to gain that type of freedom. God had other ideas in mind…

Money has always been a huge temptation for me to conquer. Not just because of the toys money can buy, but also due to the security it always seemed to bring - there is something nice about money in your pocket and having the highest view at the stop light. Unfortunately, it has always been money - or even more accurately - the desire for the selfish fruits made possible by money that led me from the Lord.

For the last two and a half years, God has freed my wife and I from this temptation. Re-entering the ministry as a middle-aged "Missionary" first freed us from possessing money, then, much more slowly, freed us from being possessed by it.

The other night we sat with a small group of adults in our church. The topic was discerning God's will for our lives and eventually the topic moved onto possessions and money. Never before had I put the equation together, but that night a formula for God's will came to me like a searchlight in my face.

In the last two years, since our lives have been simplified so much, God's will has never been clearer in my life. Never before could I hear his words so clearly, see his signs so readily or hear his promises so accurately. With fervor, I found myself praising and thanking God for this gift of freedom and clarity - and passionately pleading that God would help me love and embrace this simplicity forever.

Simplicity of life = clarity of God's will.

The voices of other God's are so loud, Lord. They cry out in television commercials, in flashy advertisements in sparkling gold and chrome. Your voice remains constant, but all too often, in my stupidity, I cannot hear it. I am like a man who lives next to the railroad tracks and can no longer hear the train. Sharpen my hearing to you, Lord. Rid me of all the things that complicate my vision, my hearing, or my senses towards you - Amen.

Convenient Believer

Psalm 78

In spite of all this they went on sinning,
they did not believe in his wonders.
God ended their days abruptly,
their years in sudden death.
Psalm 78:32-33

Psalms weren't known for their length, they were mostly songs and memory poems of praise and worship. But this Psalm is a historical piece. It is the second longest Psalm providing a poetical history of the relationship between a faithful God and his wandering - even spiteful - people.

I can almost hear the faltering voice of a nervous young boy trying to recite this Psalm from memory at his Bar Mitzvah (coming of age ceremony).

This verse is critical to understanding the relationship between God and his people. God brings them out of slavery but they pined for Pharaoh's yoke. God gave them water in the wilderness but it wasn't enough, they wanted food to go with it. God gave them manna - Bread from Heaven - but they wanted meat. God gave them quail and with it, this admonition for their unfaithfulness: "To the people, however, you shall say: Sanctify yourselves for tomorrow, when you shall have meat to eat. For in the hearing of the LORD you have cried, 'Would that we had meat for food! Oh, how well off we were in Egypt!' Therefore the LORD will give you meat for food, and you will eat it, not for one day, or two days, or five, or ten, or twenty days, but for a whole month-until it comes out of your very nostrils and becomes loathsome to you. For you have spurned the LORD who is in your midst, and in his presence you have wailed, 'Why did we ever leave Egypt?'" (Numbers 11:18-20)

Yet, the more God gave to these people, the "whinier" they became. In other cases they became prideful, taking God's work to their own credit and distancing themselves from his love. In fact, the only time they would turn to God was in times of turmoil and crises. Whenever God lifted away his protecting shield - they would suddenly flip-flop and return on their hands and knees.

It is hard for me to admit, but this history is uncomfortably similar to my own. All too often, I am the 'Convenient Believer'. My personal history embarrassingly coincides with the Israelite people - running to God when He feels absent, while I lie in the cactus plants of my own consequences.

It is good for us to examine our faith in light of the history in this Psalm. When everything goes well - do I remember to be grateful? Put credit where it is due? Do I remember God's hand in adulation? Do I embrace the gift with humility or... do I whine: "Yea, you gave me bread, but where's my meat? My gravy? My veggies? My glass of Cabernet?"

Do I turn to God only in crisis? When I've rowed into a Tsunami? Or do I see him when he guides me through the safe waters, in the sun, the refreshing breeze and the beauty of the 'normal' days?

All too often, I credit myself with His successes and blame Him for my failures.

In too many ways, this Psalm is not just the history of the Jewish people, it is my personal history. I am the 'Convenient Believer'.

Save me from my pride, dear Lord. Build in me a grateful Spirit. Turn my thoughts to you and let me praise your name consistently - Amen,

Joy to the power of infinity

Psalm 147

Hallelujah!
How good to celebrate our God in song;
how sweet to give fitting praise.
Psalm 147:1

In the last Psalm, I wrote that God's greatest desire for our lives is joy. In this Psalm, God's greatest joy is also revealed to us. The greatest joy of God is our praise - exhibited through prayer, worship and… trust. Verse eleven goes on to state; "The Lord delights in those who fear him (show him reverence), who put their hope in his unfailing trust."

I melt at the trust in my children's eyes. In their eyes, I am protector, source of strength and sustenance, unfailing love. As they grow, they will inevitably see the frailties of their old man. I detect that many parents - especially fathers - are threatened by this inevitability. However, I praise God that this does not at all frighten me. It raises no fear in me because I consider myself to be only a way point. My imperfect love is only a sign towards a stronger love; one that is truly worthy of the childlike trust they now place in me. This I pray with all my heart will be my greatest gift to them. I want them to remember how much I love them, but - even more - I want them to remember me as the one who showed them God's love.

That is joy without end - Joy to the Power of Infinity. To know that this is also God's greatest joy - his will for my life - is the hiatus of my hope, my opus, my mountain peak. It amazes me, overwhelms me, that this joy which I imperfectly experience is also God's most precious joy. It is the sign of the Creator's touch within my heart; deep calling to deep, like calling to like. It is my stream to his river, his rain to my parched tongue. It reverberates within my soul like a crystal bell; it lifts me upwards like a heavenly chorus. It brings tears of joy to my eyes as I watch my children outgrow their toys, their clothes, their beds, and eventually, their understanding that though their father was not perfect in life, he was perfected by love.

I praise God for this gift of joy. I praise God that this joy, manifested in worship and trust, is his joy as well.

Unite me joy in your joy, Lord. Let me taste your love with all my senses. Let me praise you with all my being. Let my joy be evident to all - but especially to my own family constantly, continually - Amen.

One more sneeze
Psalm 9

The LORD is a stronghold for the oppressed,
a stronghold in times of trouble.
Those who honor your name trust in you;
you never forsake those who seek you, LORD.
Psalm 9:10-11

The apostle Paul gives thanks for the strangest things. Writing to the Corinthians, he tells them of the many times he was beaten, whipped, stoned and in danger for the sake of the Lord. In his letter to the Philippians, he tells them to "Rejoice" because the Lord is near. He praises God for meeting his needs when he possessed much and when he had nothing. And all this praising is done under house arrest in Nero's cruel Rome.

All too often my understanding of suffering is missing breakfast, waiting in a long line at the checkout stand or having my airplane delayed because of weather. I cannot imagine the heights of Paul's faith - yet - perhaps that's because I cannot imagine the depths of Paul's suffering.

As I write this, I am midway through a 14-hour bus ride, heading home from Colon, Mexico having spent the last ten days at an orphanage. Deep in my chest is an aching cough complicated by a throbbing earache. I know where I caught this virus, I can pinpoint the moment. I was sitting in the middle of a bunch of giggling three to six year old girls. Some were examining my wristwatch; others were using my body as a monkey gym. Four or five more were covering my eyes and playing, "guess who?" There were sweaty little hands, runny little noses and the sounds of coughing and sneezing all around me. And, in the midst of it (though it was really hard to hear) was the sound of my heart breaking.

The wonders of a virus... For ten days we shared space, food, tables, stories and, of course, this bothersome pathogenic bug. Still, I would not trade this hacking cough for even one of those hugs. I wouldn't trade it for any one of those giggles. When I think: "Which smile would I leave behind in exchange for this cold? Which nose would I not wipe? Which goodnight kiss would I give back to rid myself of this little cough?" The answer is simply; "None."

Paul felt true suffering, but never felt forsaken. There's often a difference between the Lord's concept of "forsaken" and my concept of the word. When my heart is closed to love; when I am centered in myself; conscious of only my needs or pain then I feel persecuted, forsaken.

When I give my suffering to love (or receive suffering because of love) I find, tucked in the recesses of the pain like a pearl in an oyster, an immeasurable gift of faith and compassion.

Without you, I am truly forsaken and all life is suffering, but through you, even the worst suffering can lead to a deeper appreciation of life. I do not seek to suffer, Lord. But I do seek to love. Lord, if I do suffer because of love, please let it lead me closer to you - Amen.

Creation's Choir

Psalm 148

Let them all praise the LORD'S name;
for the LORD commanded and they were created.
Psalm 148:5

God's will for us is to praise Him; His joy in us is when we praise Him. In fact, this Psalm lays bare that the whole of all creation, the alpha, the omega, the heights and the depths, each creature, every star, all that exists… We Are The Choir of Creation!
Years ago (it seems like lifetimes ago) when I was a musician, one of the songs that I wrote was about the Creation Choir. Its tune was very simple, the theme often inter- twining with Beethoven's 'Ode to Joy'.
"Listen, listen expectedly, soon at the break of a new day, listen. Listen, listen purposefully, soon you will see the sun rise and then listen."
"The grass is still bathed by the dew. Glittering emeralds that dance with the sun but soon become mist as they rise to the skies then they fall again. Lord, they fall again."
"The birds are like heralds of morning, racing about with their singing."
"Dancing upon the breath of the dawn, all of them joined in this movement of song and all of movement seems as though one in an endless sea and it encompasses me. Listen…"
There are places in this world where we can experience this chorus. It seems to depend more on what I bring to those places than on what already exists there. At this moment, the jet I am riding is crossing the great Rocky Mountains and I can hear this chorus. There have been times in the laughter of my children that I thought I could hear angels harmonize. Sipping coffee in an outdoor cafe in Guatemala; meditating upon God's word while waiting for a youth on a downtown street corner; in a room touched by a child's birth; even with a family grieving a parent's death; the surroundings are inconsequential, my awareness of God's presence is all that matters.
The Creation Chorus sings at all moments - whether I hear it, or even add my voice - is indicative of my closeness to God, my involvement in praise; in prayer.

My loving Creator, in all life your precious creation sings harmonies of praise to your holy name. Sometimes in a minor key, a key of sadness and compassion. Sometimes in grand majors, with gusto and joy. Tune me to your orchestra, help my voice add beauty to your choir - Amen.

The City of God
Psalm 48

Great is the LORD and highly praised
in the city of our God:
The holy mountain,
fairest of heights,
the joy of all the earth,
Mount Zion, the heights of Zaphon,
the city of the great king.
Psalm 48:2 -3

Juan has a hard job in which he takes a significant amount of pride. As the caretaker of the Mexican orphanage, he oversees three facilities meeting the physical needs of three hundred children and another thirty crippled elderly residents. He performs this miraculous slight-of-hand on a floating budget that consists of whatever funds are left after food and medical needs.

Juan not only has to be frugal - he has to be extremely creative as well.

I was honored to be invited to his house for dinner. I have to admit I was curious as to what his house would look like. It was very much as I had imagined. His house was a reflection of his soul. It was simple and clean (but not uncomfortably so) with a sense of joy floating in the atmosphere. They had lots of plants, but not an abundance of furniture. What he owned was obviously making its appearance in perhaps a second or third household, yet it was well cared for. There was obvious respect among the members of his household, consisting of his wife and there three children. We laughed, ate and talked late into the night.

At times I have often wondered what God's house will look like?

I would guess that all we need to do is examine His works and they would tell us of His character and the place where He would call home. This is a God who signed the covenant with Noah with a rainbow. Consider water - the oceans, the lakes and streams and how they all interact. Consider the mountains, the forests, the deserts and all the creatures that abide in each different biosphere. Think of how the whole system interacts and complements each component, down to the microcosmic detail, even on a subatomic level. Then, dwell on the universe and the billions of galaxies, planets, and stars. Consider their patterns of passing, the complexity of their interdependency and yet, the relative simplicity of the rules by which all of this is assembled.

This will tell you about God. Immense, powerful, awesome, wondrous and yet, all that He has created works together towards an interlocking purpose. Each body supports and sustains the other bodies - not in a static sculpture - but in an elaborate and interdependent dance. Each molecule, every force drives towards a further perfection. Harmony, Integrity, wondrous beauty, wholeness in creation, holiness in our Creator.

Juan's house was so simple and yet, so complex. The furniture was threadbare, but the people were bound together by a love that man could not tear. The house represented the owner. Similarly, God's house represents its owner. It is knitted together by forces so subtle that the naked eye cannot see them. Yet, it is so strong that neither can we break them without creating without breaking unimaginable links. Look at His home and see His majesty. Take a moment to worship in awe of the Lord.

Welcome to the home of God!

No planet centers on itself, Lord. Each interacts with the others, moons to planets, planets to suns, suns to galaxies. Keep me interacting, Lord. Keep me ever-looking out toward you, responsive toward your 'gravitational pull' within in my heart - Amen.

Evil & Live

Psalm 54

Turn back the evil upon my foes;
in your faithfulness, destroy them.
Psalm 54:7

M. Scott Peck, famous author, speaker and renowned psychiatrist, says that to do 'evil' is to 'live' backwards. Instead of falling in love with that which brings joy, we fall in love with that which brings death. Instead of embracing 'living beings' we embrace 'lifeless things'.

Peck believes we do this because we can't control beings like we can control things. When you are with the living, stuff happens; spontaneity, creativity and tragedy. Because we so overwhelmingly fear losing control, we push away the living and guard ourselves with physical and spiritual walls of the dead; property, fences, investments, insurance, laws and a myriad assortment of status symbols.

Howard Hughes, Elvis Presley and Michael Jackson would be the best examples of this in contemporary times. The wealthier they became, the stranger they became, until they became as infamous for their oddities as they were famous for their wealth.

But, in smaller ways, most of us lean toward these behaviors to the extent that our means allows us. We wall ourselves away from the surrounding community if possible; moving to the country, moving from intercultural areas. (I live in a county with the second highest 'flight' rate in of the United States - people fleeing this county because of the increased cultural mix).

Yet, these actions have a way of recoiling on our very souls. The worst part is how isolated we become from the very ones with whom God would have us share our faith. Instead of freeing us, it spiritually isolates us.

To be a Christian, I think we must constantly ask ourselves not only; "What would Jesus do?" We must also ask; "Where would Jesus do it?"

"Where would Jesus go in your community?"

Wherever there is pain - you will find Jesus. Wherever people are impoverished - you will find Jesus. Wherever there is hunger, tragedy, injustice - these are the places Jesus could be found. Is it difficult to assume that these are the very places where he can still be found today?

To find Jesus we must not flee this pain. We must go towards it. This is what it means to 'live'. When we flee, when we wrap ourselves in the cloak of materialism, we embrace evil. Our lives are strangled with each attempt at control.

The call of Jesus to "follow me," would lead us out of control, away from things, and back into the fullness of what it means to truly 'alive'.

Live in me, Lord. Help me embrace my trust in you to point out those things you would find material and temporal. Make them become abhorrent to me. Encourage me, Holy Spirit. Make my path toward Jesus be a path that deepens my faith and joy with every step I take away from 'things' and towards 'beings' - Amen.

An egg facial
Psalm 70

Let those who say "Aha!"
turn back in their shame.
Psalm 70:4

Two days ago, on Memorial Day, we took one of our youth teams fishing. Early in the morning a group of our kids showed up at our church with fishing poles (and numerous creative varieties of fishing gear like I have never seen).

It is difficult to say this with etiquette, but we live in a town that still thinks 'white' yet, the population of our schools is 84% Hispanic under the age of thirty. In our little red-necked community, whenever a group of Hispanic youth gather, it looks suspicious to many people. Apparently - even when the gathering is at a church.

It was the second time this school year that a cadre of police officers arrive at our doorstep with weapons drawn. With the exception of our Catholic neighbors it is an interesting comment on our churches that non-white youth attending a church would be considered so unusual. Of course you can add to the existing suspicions the fishing rods that the kids brought. Apparently, the kid's fishing rods looked enough like guns to alarm the man who called the officers.

When everything had calmed down, I sat down with the kids - who were quite angry. It was an anger that I was not going to deny. I've now been in too many situations with them to say that racism and prejudicial attitudes are dead. This was just a small taste of hostility that I have seen displayed so far since my arrival in this County (the 11th most violent County in the United States).

The youth reaction was to place the entire blame on the cops - which also wasn't right in this circumstance. I told the kids that the police were called and had to respond (albeit, perhaps not so enthusiastically). We finally agreed that if anyone should be wearing egg for a facial it should be the man across the street in his truck who had called the police. He sat there throughout the whole ordeal with a video camera waiting to watch the action break out between the quick-draw Police Officers and our teen gang of fly-casting fishermen (and women). When the action dispersed without out so much as a worm cast or a bobber detonated; he sped away looking sullen and disappointed. It was not going to be his lucky week to preview his video on another reality TV show.

It seems so rare that I actually get to watch the one saying, 'aha', also catch his breath and say, 'oops.' Each of us occasionally wonders where the State Patrolman is when the lunatic in the car ahead of us cuts us off. However, for the kids it was just another day of asking; "Is this because I'm Hispanic?"

And sadly, I could not honestly tell them, "No."

As for me, I have come to believe that one of my primary jobs is to catch these kids doing things right and the more I do that, the more 'right' things I see them do. My prayer is that we can catch kids doing right more and more often, at younger and younger ages. I pray our "Aha, aha," moments become moments of empowerment and praise creating new images of pride and competence.

My heart is so full of pre-judgments, Lord, that my sight is tinted with fear. Help my actions transcend my vision. Every time someone breaks the barrier of my preconceptions with an act of kindness, my vision is proved wrong. Lord, please keep proving me wrong - Amen.

Acknowledgments

When thanks are given, it is often easier to be grateful in word to God than grateful in deed to the ones that He sends us. Having no desire to fail on this account, I want first to thank my wife and my children. You have daily bore the burden of mission with me through all of these years.

We have jokingly spoke of bread for the journey when, in fact, we didn't know how we would put bread on the table that very day. Yet, we always fed together upon the richest things; the inmate who found God living in his cell, the child who found their dignity in a start-up business, the dying invalid whose hand we held during her last breaths. However, above all, we have dined upon each other's home-cooked love. And it was goOOod.

Thank you, Tracey, Taylor, Amanda and Darlene for gracing whatever form of bread God laid upon our table.

Thank you also to Gene who determined to publish this book even before he read it. Gene believed in me enough to 'fix' the book because I was more important to him than even the words that I had written. You don't find friends like that – they are given to you.

Finally, I want to acknowledge that my life is filled with stories because my life is filled with people. In this book are stories of my family, my friends and the people whose pain and joy I have been allowed to share. Every one of them introduced God to me in a fuller and richer way. My dear Lord, Jesus, to the extent that my life has been any sort of blessing to others – it is because you blessed me with these lives.

I pray Lord that you would continue to give me the courage to be found with the lost and not lost with the found.

Invitation to Ministry

Jerry would like to extend an invitation for you to join him in ongoing ministry. There are many ways that you can participate – as you are called.

First, of course, is to love like Jesus loved. The vulnerable live in your own neighborhood. The harvest is full, but too many of us get too comfy in the grain elevators. If you are unsure of how to engage and empower the vulnerable in your own community; we would like to serve as a resource.

ONEFAMILY OUTReach offers training, workshops, retreats, concerts or just support through e-mail, letters and prayers to any who seek to serve Jesus in his most vulnerable form. In addition, Jerry offers a weekly newsletter and in-depth bible study that is designed to both inform and motivate those who seek to: "Do justice, love mercy, and walk humbly with their God."

We can also offer support to those who want to develop directional friendships with people seeking to recover their lives. If you are interested in outreach to the incarcerated, homeless, or at-risk youth we hope you will find us a trusted friend and resource.

Finally, we seek interns who are interested in helping us with innovative, hands-on ministry to the vulnerable (with a primary – but not exclusive – focus on at-risk youth). This work includes starting small business projects, endurance athletics and leadership development. If this interests you, please contact Jerry personally.

jerry goebel
ONEFAMILY OUTReach
http://OneFamilyOutreach.com
jerry@OneFamilyOutreach.com